Insights into Bible Times and Customs

by G. Christian Weiss

Director of Missions
Back to the Bible Broadcast

A BACK TO THE BIBLE PUBLICATION

Back to the Bible
Lincoln, Nebraska 68501

118,000 printed to date—1977
(5-6468—3M—67)
ISBN 0-8474-1281-4

Printed in the United States of America

Foreword

The pages of Scripture are alive with illustrations from everyday life in the Middle East. To appreciate these allusions to daily life, one must have some understanding of the times and customs of the Middle East when the Bible was written.

Recognizing the importance of this knowledge to Bible readers, the *Good News Broadcaster* began a column in 1968 entitled Insights Into Bible Times and Customs. G. Christian Weiss was selected to write this column because he is so well qualified in this field. Not only has he been a careful Bible student all of his adult life, but he has also lived in the Middle East as a missionary, where he had opportunity to view firsthand many of these customs which are still followed in that part of the world.

The column proved to be of much interest to *Broadcaster* readers. Many requested that the material be put in book form for easier reference; thus, we have produced this book with the same title as the column.

We are confident that your appreciation of the Bible will increase as you read this book and gain more insight into Bible times and customs.

—Harold J. Berry
Literature Editor

Contents

Animals of the Bible

Chapter 1

Old Garment—New Cloth

When the Pharisees criticized Jesus for socializing with publicans and sinners, and when they compared the conduct of His disciples with that of John's disciples, Jesus casually said, "No man putteth a piece of new cloth unto an old garment" (Matt. 9:16). To get the full picture, read Matthew 9:14-16, Mark 2:18-21 and Luke 5:33-36.

The cloth Jesus was talking about was raw, handwoven, all-wool fabric. When a garment made of such cloth is subjected to washings and exposed to the elements, a phenomenal amount of change and shrinking takes place. A radical alteration in the texture and a drastic reduction in size occur.

But once the garment has been aged and completely shrunk to final size and condition, sewing a patch of new and unshrunken material on it for the purpose of mending a tear or worn spot becomes utterly unfeasible—unthinkable, really. The new cloth, upon exposure to the elements, will radically shrink in size and change in texture, further tearing the old garment in the process. As Jesus said, "The rent is made worse." He was stating that which was perfectly obvious to His

7

hearers and with which they would all readily agree.

What is the spiritual significance of this figure of speech? Jesus was speaking of the Pharisees, the religious conservatives of their day. These men were clinging to the "old garment" of their own self-righteousness and ritualistic religion—the forms, the fastings, the making of prayers, and so on. They could readily accept and endorse the ministry of John the Baptist, the prophet whose ministry was marked by austerity and asceticism. They said to Jesus, "The disciples of John fast often, and make prayers" (Luke 5:33). This was where they excelled. This was the "old cloth" they were clinging to—the old garment of self-righteousness. Theirs was a religion of works and rites.

Human righteousness in itself, though perhaps admired by defective human vision, is, in the eyes of God, as abhorrent and repulsive as the "filthy rags" to which it is compared in Isaiah 64:6.

But Jesus did not come with the same "old cloth." He did not display or place merit on fasting, making long prayers in public, disfiguring the face in false religious pretense, or any such thing. He came with something new to offer men. He had new doctrines, a new manner and new matter in His teaching, as well as new grace, new bread and water, a new birth and a new life (Mark 1:22,27; 11:18).

The Pharisees were not prepared to accept Christ's new doctrines. They questioned His authority, repudiated His claims and rejected His teachings. They might have been willing to take some of His teachings and patch them onto their old religious garments, but Jesus told them that this could not be done.

Christ was introducing a new joy and freedom of soul, which He Himself was bringing into the world, the opposite of human self-righteousness and of the spirit of religious legalism. The Pharisees could not understand this. Jesus made the spiritual truth of His mission utterly clear to them by an illustration they could readily grasp. He had brought new life and liberty to the souls of publicans and sinners.

It was after Matthew had accepted His invitation to follow Him that Jesus dined in the tax collector's house. Jesus made it clear to His critics, the Pharisees, that His gospel of grace and spiritual restoration was incompatible with their self-righteousness.

People today are still trying to "patch" their old, filthy garments with bits of the gospel—with the rite of baptism, the making of prayers, church membership, religious observances, and so on. But God doesn't accept a few "new" patches on man's old, defective garment. He extends to us a completely new garment, made of the spotless righteousness of Jesus Christ, His Son—"the garments of salvation, . . . the robe of righteousness" (Isa. 61:10). This new garment is able to cover all man's sin and nakedness and fit him for the eternal, holy fellowship of God.

Patchwork becomes incongruous in appearance and utterly incompatible in essence. But the garment which Christ gives—the garment of righteousness—makes one acceptable to men, to the angels of heaven and to God Himself.

Chapter 2

Old Bottles—New Wine

"No man," said Jesus, "putteth new wine into old bottles; else the new wine will burst the bottles, and be spilled, and the bottles shall perish. But new wine must be put into new bottles; and both are preserved" (Luke 5:37,38; see also Matt. 9:17; Mark 2:22).

This "parable" is parallel to that of the new cloth and the old garment, and it conveys essentially the same meaning. It is a vivid figure of speech and cannot fail to convict anyone familiar with it.

To the Westerner there is no real significance to the age of a bottle. Old or new, our glass bottles have essentially the same strength. We return our empty pop bottles to the store and get the refund of our deposit. The bottles are used repeatedly, almost indefinitely. And why not? An old bottle is as good as a new one.

Present-day industry has no real concern over the age of the bottles wine is put into, only that each bottle be safely sealed. Why then did Jesus say that no man puts new wine into old bottles, but new wine must be put into new bottles?

The "bottles" Jesus was referring to were not glass bottles, such as we are accustomed to, but wineskins—goatskins or sheepskins which were used in His time for carrying water and storing wine. After the animal was killed, air was blown under the skin through a quill or straw to separate the skin from the carcass. The carcass was then pulled out of the skin, which remained intact except for the openings left when the head and feet were severed. These were tied securely, and the skin formed a perfect bag or "bottle."

I often saw water carriers in Morocco with a sheepskin or a goatskin slung over their shoulders by a rope or strap, going about in the streets or marketplaces selling drinking water to thirsty people.

Skin bottles are referred to numerous times in the Scriptures (see Gen. 21:14; Josh. 9:4,13; Ps. 119:83). The English word "bottles" is a somewhat misleading translation; the accurate rendering of the Hebrew word is "skins."

This background gives real meaning to Jesus' figure of speech. A new, fresh wineskin would be flexible and elastic enough to stretch under the pressure of fermenting wine, whereas an old, stiff one would simply burst apart and result in destruction of both the "bottle" and the wine. Jesus' teaching was that Christianity cannot be contained in ancient Judaism; nor can grace be confined in the bonds of legalism.

The Pharisees had countenanced the preaching of John and were to some extent at least amenable to his austerity and asceticism. They endorsed his practices of fasting frequently and of praying, while questioning Jesus' teaching and emphasis on

11

freedom and joy. They asked, "Why do the disciples of John fast often, and make prayers, and likewise the disciples of the Pharisees; but thine eat and drink?" (Luke 5:33).

Jesus answered in effect: "I have brought new wine to my disciples. I have brought new life to men, a new birth, a new nature, new joy and new blessings, and the new gospel that I am bringing cannot be mixed into, or confined to, rigid legalism and dead formalism. You have but a form of godliness. You are like whitewashed sepulchres, attractive in outward appearance but inwardly filled with death and corruption. The new life and joy I have brought to the world cannot be contained in these dead forms" (see Matt. 23:27).

Jesus told the seeking rabbi, Nicodemus of Jerusalem, that he must be "born again" and receive a completely new life and new nature in order to enter the kingdom of God: "Except a man be born again, he cannot see the kingdom of God" (John 3:3).

The new wine of Christ's salvation—of eternal life—and the new, unspeakable joy of that salvation could never be poured into the old, unregenerate heart of the natural man, for it would burst and demolish it. Man must be given a new heart, a new nature, a new spirit; he must become a "new creature," as the Apostle Paul avows is the case with all who are "in Christ" (II Cor. 5:17; see also Ezek. 36:26,27; Eph. 4:24; Heb. 10:16,17).

The new wine of the gospel cannot be put into the old skin of unregenerate lives and of dead religious formalism—all these old things must pass away and all things be made new. And this is exactly what Jesus came to do: "Behold, all things are become new" (II Cor. 5:17). When a person receives Christ into his life as Lord and Saviour, he receives a new heart, a new life, a new nature, new power, new joy, a new walk, a new hope, new peace, new desires, new delights—in short, *all* things become new.

The natural man does not receive the new wine of the Spirit. Spiritual things are foolish and unpalatable to him. Unconverted persons frequently try to place some select parts of the gospel into their religious curriculum. Then they try to mix Christ with ritualism and legalism in the hope of achieving the favor of God, but satisfactory results are impossible.

"No man also having drunk old wine straightway desireth new: for he saith, The old is better" (Luke 5:39). How true this is to life. Yet apart from the new birth and new life from Christ, no one can find true salvation or true inner satisfaction. Mere religion is not enough. Legalistic righteousness is inadequate (Matt. 5:20). No mere religious rite or association is of any importance. All that matters is the new creation—the result of the new birth.

Chapter 3

God Does Not Mock Prayer

In Luke 11 we find Jesus' principal teaching about prayer. The first four verses give His instructions about how men ought to pray: (1) with humility—"Our Father" (as a helpless son to an able parent); (2) with reverence—"Hallowed be thy name"; (3) with submission—"Thy will be done"; (4) with dependence and trust—"Give us this day our daily bread"; (5) with penitence— "Forgive us our debts, as we forgive our debtors"; and (6) with holy aspirations—"Lead us not into temptation, but deliver us from evil."

The next four verses record Jesus' parable about prayer, teaching us that prayer: (1) is based on a friendly relationship with God—"Shall have a friend, and shall go unto him at midnight, and shall say unto him, Friend"; (2) is to be intercession for others—"A friend of mine in his journey, is come to me"; (3) is definite and specific—"Three loaves"; (4) is done with earnest desperation—"I have nothing to set before him"; (5) is always importunate—The man knocked at "midnight"; he pressed his claim and "because of his importunity," his friend supplied his need; and (6) is gloriously rewarded—"As many [much] as he needeth."

Following the parable, Jesus proceeded to *exhort* men to be earnest and importunate in prayer. We are to ask, seek and knock with unfaltering faith and determination.

In this connection Jesus posed three somewhat strange questions: (1) "If a son ask bread of . . . a father, will he give him a stone?"; (2) "Or if he ask a fish, will he for a fish give him a serpent?"; and (3) "Or if he shall ask an egg, will he offer him a scorpion?" (vv. 11,12).

Why did Jesus ask these particular questions? Why were bread and stones contrasted? Fish and serpents? Eggs and scorpions?

The loaves of bread familiar to the people to whom Jesus was speaking were round, flattish and rather dark in color. They were made of whole wheat or barley and were baked beside an open fire in a brick oven, often being covered with ash and cinders. Hence, they actually had very much the same appearance as an ordinary stone on the ground might have had. If one of those loaves were placed amid stones of similar size, a person would probably be unable to tell at a casual glance which was bread and which was stone.

Jesus' question thus was "Would a father mock his hungry son by offering him one of the stones of the earth which have an appearance much like that of a loaf of bread?" His meaning was "Neither will God deceive His praying children by giving them something that looks like an answer to their prayers but which is in reality a cruel, mocking stone! The Heavenly Father will never mock the prayers of His children."

The comparison between a fish and a serpent is similar. There are certain types of slender, edible fish which closely resemble the deadly sea snake. An innocent child might not know the difference between them and could suffer unfortunate consequences. But God, who always knows what is true and right food for His children, will never deceive them by thrusting into their hands a serpent to beguile them when they ask for wholesome food from His hand.

But why would He associate an egg with a scorpion? This is also a vivid comparison. While many scorpions are dark in color, there is also in the Near East a light-colored variety, sometimes called the "white scorpion." Though not snow white by any means, this creature, when curled up into its relaxed state, could be mistaken for an egg. A child might pick one up, mistaking it for an egg of some kind. This would be a very serious mistake for a child to make—possibly even fatal. Jesus was saying that our Father in heaven would never deceive His children by giving them something dangerous and destructive in response to their earnest petition to Him for help in time of need. When His children ask Him for eggs, He will give them eggs. He will never deceive them by giving them a poisonous, biting scorpion.

The great lesson Jesus teaches here is that God does answer prayer. He does not mock His children. He does not deceive those who pray. He delights in giving to His children as much as they need. "Lord, teach us to pray" (Luke 11:1).

Chapter 4

Why Put Grass in an Oven?

In the Sermon on the Mount, Jesus exhorted people not to be overly concerned about this transient life: "Consider the lilies of the field, how they grow; they toil not, neither do they spin: And yet I say unto you, That even Solomon in all his glory was not arrayed like one of these. Wherefore, if God so clothe the grass of the field, which to day is, and to morrow is cast into the oven, shall He not much more clothe you, O ye of little faith? Therefore, take no thought, saying, What shall we eat? or, What shall we drink? or, Wherewithal shall we be clothed?" (Matt. 6:28-31).

While I think the basic meaning of this passage is obvious and clear to almost any person, one who has grown up in the Western world would instinctively raise the question "Why would grass be put into an oven?"

Jesus specifically speaks of "the grass of the field, which to day is, and to morrow is cast into the oven" (v. 30). What is the significance of His figure of speech?

Anyone who has lived in the Near East readily grasps the significance of this. Ovens there are heated chambers of varying shapes and sizes, made of a variety of materials such as mud, bricks, or stones. Often they are nothing more than a hollow, igloo-shaped mound of mud and cow dung with an opening on one side through which the fire is kindled and the loaves put in and taken out. The heat in the oven is generally produced by some easily ignited, quick-burning fuel, such as heavy grass or light twigs. When the fuel has burned down to a mass of hot cinders and the oven is well heated, the loaves of bread are placed in the oven and the opening is closed until the bread is thoroughly baked.

In the city the ovens are customarily large public facilities made of stones or bricks. The housewives send their leavened bread loaves to these ovens, where they are baked for a small fee and returned by "dough-boys" to the proper houses. This eliminates the necessity for a hot fire in the home and also eliminates carrying large amounts of bothersome dried grass, twigs and sticks into the houses to heat home ovens.

Jesus spoke of the beauty of the lilies of the field, calling attention to the fact that they do not toil or spin and yet are arrayed in glory surpassing that of the great King Solomon. Then He added, "Wherefore, if God so clothe the grass of the field, which to day is, and to morrow is cast into the oven, shall he not much more clothe you?" (v. 30). The lilies He referred to are flowers that grow on a rather heavy stalk with long and rather broad leaves, which when dried make ideal fuel for the baking ovens. And, of course, in the intensely hot sun these stalks and leaves dry quickly so that the lilies might indeed be blooming in the field one day and a day or two later their "grass" could be serving as fuel in the ovens. This was well known to His hearers.

Our earthly lives in comparison to eternity and in relation to spiritual considerations are so brief and insignificant as to be likened to "grass of the field, which to day is, and to morrow is cast into the oven" (v. 30). This being the case, why should the children of God spend so much time worrying about this brief and comparatively insignificant side of life? Why should there be so much worry and concern and labor for this short journey from the cradle to the grave? Why is there not more concern for the kingdom of God and His righteousness and less anxiety for this brief existence on earth? And, most important, why should the Christian not trust God for his every need, day by day?

Since God takes such magnificent care of the transient "grass" as to adorn these stalks with beautiful flowers, is this not evidence that He will also take care of His own children? Then why should we be worried? All flesh is like this grass; though some, in the endowments of body and mind, are like lilies, beautiful and much admired, still they are but grass. We, accordingly, should take no anxious thought for the future, concerning what we should wear, because perhaps by tomorrow we may be dressed in our graveclothes.

Consider also how free the lilies are from care; they do not toil as men do to earn their clothing and nourishment; neither do they spin, as women do to make their garments. Yet consider how fair and how fine the lilies are! Note how they grow and what form they have; out of the obscurity of the ground, in a few weeks they come to be so beautiful that even Solomon in all his glory could not be compared to them. Let us, therefore, desire the wisdom of Solomon rather than the glory of Solomon, in which he was outdone by the lilies of the field. Knowledge and grace are the perfection of man, not beauty, and much less, fine clothes.

Jesus' parable teaches us not to have anxious care for clothing, not to covet it, and not to be proud of it, because at best we cannot dress as finely as do the lilies of the field, and our adorning, like theirs, will soon perish.

This brings to mind the exhortation written by the Apostle John: "Love not the world, neither the things that are in the world. The world passeth away, and the lust thereof: but he that doeth the will of God abideth for ever" (I John 2:15,17).

Chapter 5

The Barren Fig Tree

Jesus' pronouncement of judgment upon a certain barren fig tree was not a fit of anger; rather, it was for the purpose of teaching His disciples—and all men—a solemn spiritual lesson (Mark 11:12-14,20,21). We must bear this in mind whenever we talk about "the barren fig tree."

But what was the significance of the barren fig tree upon which Jesus pronounced a curse and judgment?

Fig trees produce two distinct fruits. In the Arabic language, which is the universal tongue of the Holy Land and the rest of the Middle East, these two fruits are known by completely different names. The "early figs" are called *baakoor*, while the regular figs, with which we are most familiar, are called *kirmoos*.

Figs of the early variety mature in the spring, from the end of March through April and May; the others mature in late summer or autumn. The *baakoor* cannot be left to ripen on the tree and then be dried and used in the manner of the regular figs. They must be eaten directly from the tree in what might be called their "green" state. They are very soft and puffy and exceedingly sweet—

sickeningly so to the uninitiated person. These first, crude, untimely figs are of no commercial value, but they are often plucked and eaten by passersby.

Another significant thing about the fig tree is that the early fruit appears before the leaves. (Fig leaves, when fully matured, are very large in size and of rather heavy texture). If the early figs have not appeared by the time the leaves are developed, it is a sound conclusion that they will not grow on that tree. This was the condition Jesus encountered when He was traveling with His disciples. The fig tree they saw had already developed its leaves, and they naturally expected to find the sweet, first-produced figs (the *baakoor*). But though the tree had an abundance of leaves, giving promise of fruit, it proved to be a hypocritical tree. It would obviously remain barren. Jesus pronounced judgment upon it, and the next day His disciples marveled when they saw that the fig tree had "dried up from the roots" (Mark 11:20). The marvel of the miracle becomes all the greater when one remembers that the Palestinian fig tree was not merely a small plant or shrub but rather a sizable tree that did not bear fruit until it was a few years old and that grew to a height of 20 feet or more.

Both the word and the act of Jesus were intended to be parabolic. Jesus despised hypocrisy. He constantly condemned profession without productivity—without "fruits." This fig tree, by its show of leaves, should also have had fruit; but its leaves were only an empty, false profession.

The nation of Israel is frequently referred to in the Bible as being like a fig tree. Jesus came to this nation, "to His own," expecting to find spiritual

22

fruit. He should have found in these people the traits of godliness, righteousness, love, faith and obedience to God's Word. Instead, He found hypocrisy, deadness, empty profession, forms of godliness without reality or power, and pride rather than penitence and faith. The hypocritical fig tree afforded Him a splendid opportunity to vividly portray the state of the nation. And His judgment upon the tree was indicative of the judgment of God that would soon fall on them. That judgment fell on the nation in A.D. 70, when the city of Jerusalem was conquered and sacked by the Roman armies and the people were dispersed for two long millennia. The special tree of Jehovah's planting and prolonged care was put under divine judgment. As a nation it "dried up from the roots" and remained barren.

It is only because of God's grace that this nation did not die and fade away. But Jesus Himself promised shortly after this episode that this "fig tree" would revive and bud again. In many places the Bible predicts that the nation will be resurrected and restored and become spiritually productive again; many Old Testament prophecies plainly imply this, and Paul's New Testament treatise in Romans 11 puts it beyond doubt.

Individuals also need to take the lesson of the barren fig tree to heart. God hates and universally condemns hypocrisy, no matter where it is found.

Does not the Church today resemble the barren fig tree, having leaves without fruit and profession without productivity?

Chapter 6

The Camel and the Needle's Eye

What was Jesus actually saying in Luke 18:25, when He said, "It is easier for a camel to go through a needle's eye, than for a rich man to enter into the kingdom of God"?

Various interpretations have been given to His statement. When I first heard the explanation that "needle's eye" was the name of a certain type of gate known to people in the Holy Land, I wondered whether this actually was what Jesus referred to or whether this was a fanciful modern interpretation of Scripture to take some of the bluntness away from Jesus' statement and to make it more palatable to rich people. But the question was settled in my mind while I was in the Holy Land a few years ago.

A Syrian guide was taking me through the city of Damascus on a tour. We came to a section of what apparently had been a very ancient wall, and he called my attention to the nature of the huge wooden gates. Then he pointed to a small, low door beside the main gate, and I was struck forcibly with this statement: "That is what is called the 'needle's eye.' "

I had read about the smaller gates beside the large city gates of ancient cities, made to allow travelers to enter or leave the city at night when the large main gates were barred fast and could not be opened except by special permit from the head man of the city. Now, in the ancient city of Damascus, I actually heard such a gate being called a "needle's eye." I was convinced. The Jaffa gate in Jerusalem also has a very fine example of one of these small "needle's eye" entrances.

Jesus had been speaking to the rich young ruler who wanted to enter the kingdom of God but was unwilling to loosen his grip on worldly wealth and material possessions. Jesus had told him that he lacked one thing: "Sell all that thou hast, and distribute unto the poor, and thou shalt have treasure in heaven: and come, follow me" (v. 22). When the young man heard this, "he was very sorrowful: for he was very rich" (v. 23). Jesus then sadly added the comment, "How hardly shall they that have riches enter into the kingdom of God! For it is easier for a camel to go through a needle's eye, than for a rich man to enter into the kingdom of God" (v. 25).

Picture the metaphor Jesus used. Camels loaded with sacks of grain, wood, charcoal, or other commodities entered the city daily. If a merchant should happen to arrive in the evening after the main gates of the city were closed, the only way he and his beast could possibly enter would be for the camel to be unloaded of all of its baggage and made to kneel and literally crawl through the "needle's eye" on his knees. Stripped bare and down on its knees! The clear implication is that a wealthy man, in order to become a Chris-

25

tian, must be ready to let go of his material wealth and humble himself to the level of a poverty-stricken sinner at the feet of Jesus. The rich young man would not do this; hence, he could not enter.

Nothing is too hard for God to achieve in a human soul. When men are at a loss, God is not. Many a rich man has met the terms of Christ and entered into the kingdom of heaven bereft of all dependence on material assets and humbly kneeling at the foot of the cross. A good New Testament example is Zaccheus. This man gloriously released his grasp on wealth and material assets, relieved himself of the burden of a guilty conscience, and humbly repented of his sinful life to join the fellowship of Jesus Christ, his Saviour and Master.

Chapter 7

Leaky Ceilings and Quarrelsome Women

"A continual dropping in a very rainy day and a contentious woman are alike" (Prov. 27:15). This statement by Solomon embraces both wit and wisdom. The man had a vast measure of both. Unfortunately, he also displayed a disturbing measure of folly, though it may be that some of his wisdom actually accrued from his follies.

The Book of Proverbs reveals the wisdom which Solomon obtained, not only through pursuit of study (Eccles. 1:16,17) but also through long and vast experience, much of which was exceedingly bitter. This book also reveals that in his later life the king saw his folly. Proverbs contains many strong and solemn warnings to younger men against the very follies that had marred his own life (see Prov. 1:10-20; 5:1-23; 6:23-28; 7:6-27; 9:14-18; 22:14). The Book of Proverbs indicates that Solomon repented of his foolish and sinful sensuality before his death and that he was restored to a life of righteousness and fellowship with God.

The statement "A continual dropping in a very rainy day and a contentious woman are alike" illustrates a bitter lesson Solomon learned from his multiplied relationships with women. What a holocaust of jealousies, quarrelings and bitter contentions his house must have been!

What is the meaning of Solomon's declaration?

The houses in that area of the world have changed little in design since Solomon's day. They are commonly constructed with flat, thick, mud roofs covered with a heavy coating of lime and whitewash to prevent the rain from penetrating and soaking through the mud. The rafters or beams of the houses are made of durable timber placed close together to sustain the great weight of the heavy roof. A layer of thinner boards is laid over these rafters, and then heavy, wet soil is solidly tamped over the top, layer after layer, sometimes to the thickness of 18 or 20 inches. This type of construction greatly aids in keeping the houses cool in the hotter seasons of the year and warm in colder weather.

If the coat of whitewash on the surface of the roof is not kept in good condition, cracks develop, and on a very rainy day will penetrate the soil beneath. After hours of prolonged rainfall, the water will start dripping through the ceiling below. Pity the occupant when that happens, because long after the rain has subsided, the dripping continues. It will continue for many hours after the storm, even for days. And there is nothing that can be done to stop the dripping once the mud has become saturated.

Solomon lived under such a roof. He also lived with a large number of contentious women, and he knew that experience too.

A contentious and quarrelsome woman continues to nag and fume over a disagreement long after the storm has passed, like the "continual dropping" from a faulty roof. Some women remain moody, bitter and unyielding with their husbands and families for days following what was but a temporary storm. When the "violent rain" (as Peter Lange translates it) ceased, the whole thing should have been over, but with a quarrelsome woman it is not so. Pity the man whose wife is like the "continual dropping" of a leaky Eastern roof!

The next verse goes on to say, "Whosoever hideth her hideth the wind, and the ointment of his right hand, which bewrayeth itself." This apparently means that whoever tries to restrain an ill-tempered woman or conceal her faults may as well try to confine the wind or to stop it from blowing or try to conceal the ointment on his hand, which signifies its presence by its odor.

Why should anyone continue to stir up trouble after the storm has subsided? Why continue the "dropping" for hours or days afterward? Why make life miserable for oneself and one's family over some temporary, though stormy, spat?

Homes of godly kindness and genuine love are the bulwark of the Church and the fortress of the nation. Mothers and wives in particular play a solemn role in making the home either pleasant or miserable.

The writer of Proverbs makes a significant number of references to contentious and discontented women, having learned the seriousness of

29

these characteristics in a wife: "A foolish son is the calamity of his father [men can be as guilty of folly as women]: and the contentions [quarrelsomeness, irritability, naggings] of a wife are a continual dropping" (19:13). Reference is made here, too, to the prolonged leaking of a mud roof following a heavy rain. "It is better to dwell in the wilderness, than with a contentious and an angry woman" (21:19). The writer later goes on to say, "It is better to dwell in the corner of the housetop [on the open roof without shelter overhead but walled to afford a degree of privacy], than with a brawling woman and in a wide [large and luxurious] house" (25:24).

It would not seem right to conclude these comments without including a significant quotation from the New Testament. The Apostle Paul wrote: "Wives, submit yourselves unto your own husbands, as unto the Lord. Husbands, love your wives, even as Christ also loved the church, and gave himself for it. So ought men to love their wives as their own bodies. They two shall be one flesh. Let every one of you in particular so love his wife even as himself; and the wife see that she reverence her husband" (Eph. 5:22,25,28,31,33). True love in the home—love to God and to one another—on the part of both man and wife is the secret to a happy, wholesome family.

Chapter 8

Gethsemane: the Olive Press

The word "Gethsemane" is from an old Aramaic word meaning "olive press." This name is significant in relation to Jesus' agony in the garden on the night of His arrest.

Many have tended to equate the olive press with the olive mill. I regard this to be an error. I have seen both in Bible lands, and as a result they are quite distinct in my mind.

The mill, whether for grapes or olives, is really a device for crushing. While the actual details of construction vary with individual mills, the basic design and the mode of operation are essentially the same. There is a large vat, usually hewn from stone, which is shaped with a rounded bottom on the inside, like the large, old-fashioned iron caldrons that were formerly used on farms to cook feed for animals. Placed inside this vat in an upright position is a huge, wheel-shaped stone—similar to a grindstone—with its circumference fitting the contour of the rounded bottom of the vat. In the center of this stone wheel is a large hole into which is fitted one end of a long wooden beam, or sweep. An animal (donkey, ox or camel) is then hitched to the end of the sweep and turns

31

the wheel by walking in a circle. As the great stone wheel turns round and round in the vat, the olives are crushed and mangled, and their oil is released. The same device is used to crush grapes to extract their juice. There is a drain in the vat at a certain level to allow the accumulated liquid to flow out into a lower, adjoining vat.

Following this operation, the mangled olives are put into woven straw containers shaped something like huge washtubs. These are then stacked one on the other under the press for the purpose of squeezing out every available drop of oil.

The press is an ingenious device by means of which a tremendous weight is placed on the stacked baskets of crushed fruit. A long, heavy beam, anchor-hinged at one end, is cantilevered over the stacked baskets. Hung from its far end is a huge, stone weight, perhaps weighing a ton or more. The beam is ingeniously maneuvered so that this weight, multiplied by the mechanics of the beam lever, presses down on the stacked baskets of pulp until every ounce of oil is squeezed out and drained into an adjoining stone vat. The baskets are left under the weight of the press for several days to make sure this squeezing is accomplished to the last drop.

Gethsemane was truly Jesus' "olive press." It was there in Gethsemane that the weight of human sin and guilt was vicariously placed on Him and all but crushed Him to death. The combined sin and guilt of all humanity of all time is a load too great and too heavy to be grasped by our human imaginations, and it literally crushed Him to the ground.

The "press" was so great that "his sweat was [like] great drops of blood falling down to the ground" (Luke 22:44). In His agony, He "fell on the ground, and prayed that, if it were possible, the hour might pass from him. And he said, Abba, Father . . . ; take away this cup from me" (Mark 14:35,36). But despite the pressure and the agony He felt, He still said, "Nevertheless not my will, but thine, be done. And there appeared an angel unto him from heaven, strengthening him" (Luke 22:42,43).

The Bible declares plainly that He bore our sins in His own body and the awful weight of that guilt and agony was beyond the ability of mere human flesh to endure.

A visualization of the olive press in conjunction with Gethsemane and Golgotha helps one to understand the true significance of His words: "I have a baptism to be baptized with; and how am I straitened till it be accomplished!" (12:50).

I never read about Gethsemane or meditate on it without seeing with my mind's eye the image of a stack of olive pulp under the great, stone weight of the olive press, forcing out every drop of fluid. Of Gethsemane, as well as of Golgotha, we may well pray, "O Lamb of God, bring its scene before me; Help me walk from day to day With its shadow o'er me" (Fanny J. Crosby).

Chapter 9

Equipment of the Palestinian Shepherd

The Bible abounds with symbolism pertaining to shepherds and sheep. Because the ancient Hebrews were a pastoral people, such symbolism spoke vividly to them. The application of the spiritual truths thus portrayed was easy and completely natural to them.

Jesus designated Himself as the Good Shepherd, and using this symbol, He taught some precious truths. The New Testament apostles referred to Jesus as their "Great Shepherd" and "Chief Shepherd" and regarded Him as being related to them as a shepherd is to his sheep.

In the Old Testament, Jehovah revealed Himself to His people as a Shepherd (Ps. 80:1; Isa. 40:11; Jer. 31:10; Ezek. 34:12). The chief passage that comes to mind in this connection is undoubtedly the Twenty-Third Psalm: "The Lord is my shepherd; I shall not want. He maketh me to lie down in green pastures: he leadeth me beside the still waters. . . . He leadeth me in the paths of righteousness. Thou anointest my head with oil"

(vv. 1-3,5). This is one of the richest, sweetest and most loved portions of the entire Bible.

But just what does "shepherd" say to us in our modern, mechanized age? To one raised on a farm it obviously conveys meaning that is not as readily grasped by the city dweller. To one who has been in the Bible lands and has lived in the culture of the Near East it says even more.

Let me describe briefly the usual equipment of a shepherd in Bible times and then point out some of the rich lessons we can learn, based on this knowledge.

Rod and staff. "Thy rod and thy staff they comfort me," testified David in Psalm 23:4. Why did the thought of a shepherd's rod and staff comfort the king?

Are the rod and staff identical, the same object being described by two different terms? Or is each separate and distinct? Some seem to think the terms apply to the same instruments, and, consequently, they have been intertranslated. But this is not really correct. The Hebrew words used, though similar, are definitely not identical. They obviously describe two separate items. Such passages as Jeremiah 48:17 differentiate between the two quite clearly.

The "rod" is basically a club about 30 inches in length, usually with a knob on the larger end formed from the "bulb" at the root of the little tree from which it is made. This knob might be studded with heavy-headed iron nails or even with flint, thus making it a formidable weapon. When dexterously swung by a skillful hand, it can be used to effectively maul an adversary. Or it might be flung at an enemy in somewhat the same

35

manner as a boomerang is thrown by an Australian bushman. A hole is made in the smaller, handle end, through which a cord is drawn so the rod can be hung from the shepherd's wrist or fastened to his belt.

Shepherds carry these rods for the express purpose of protecting their sheep (and themselves) from marauding animals or assaulting humans— "thieves and robbers" (John 10:8). David must have used such a rod when he killed the lion and the bear that came to attack his father's sheep (I Sam. 17:34-36). No wonder he wrote in Psalm 23 that the rod of the Lord comforted him. It gave him a sense of protection and security and, therefore, comfort.

What is the "staff?" This is a kind of walking stick, about 6 feet in length, usually plain and straight but sometimes with a fork or crook at one end. It is used to aid the shepherd in walking over the rough terrain, climbing hills or clambering over rocks. The word itself signifies a "stay" or "support." It is also used to guide the sheep or even to punish them.

A staff with a crook on the end is used by the shepherd to lift a sheep or lamb from a crevice between the dangerous rocks. It is also used to count the sheep as they pass under it while entering the fold at the close of the day. Jesus, in keeping with this, assures us that He knows His own sheep by name.

The Sling. The shepherd's sling was the device which David used in killing the giant Goliath. It was a common part of the shepherd's equipment. Of the men of Benjamin it is stated in the Scriptures that "every one could sling stones at an hair breadth, and not miss" (Judg. 20:16), indicating their skill and dexterity in the use of the sling.

The sling is a very simple device, but it is an extremely accurate and dangerous weapon. It consists of 2 woven strings about 15 or 16 inches in length, fastened to a small, diamond-shaped, leather pad or pouch. This pouch has a small slit in the middle so that when a stone is pressed into it, it closes around it like a bag. The strings are correctly fastened around the fingers and the sling is twirled round and round with great speed until, at a precise time, one of the strings is released and the stone is hurled through the air at great speed and with deadly power.

The security of the believer is guaranteed by the Great Shepherd, who will not flee when the wolves or hyenas come to attack His sheep but will protect them night and day. His "sling" will simultaneously rout the Enemy and protect His flock (see I Sam. 25:29).

The Scrip. What was Jesus referring to when He told His disciples not to take a "scrip" with them on their special mission to the cities of Israel (Matt. 10:10)? An Old Testament passage will clarify this for us. In I Samuel 17:40 we read of David, "He took his staff in his hand, and chose him five smooth stones out of the brook, and put them in a shepherd's bag which he had, even in a scrip; and his sling was in his hand."

The shepherd's scrip is a bag made of skin, carried over the shepherd's shoulder by means of a heavy cord, in which he carries his supply of bread, olives, cheese, dried figs and parched grain. Sometimes these bags are crudely made of raw skins, but quite often they are made of well-tanned and attractively dyed leather with exquisitely embroidered designs. Merchants carry their money and other valuables in scrips. Shepherds use it not only to carry supplies for their own needs but also emergency items for the care of injured or sick sheep, since they must be both physician and surgeon to their flocks.

Our Shepherd, Jesus Christ, has His "scrip" full of emergency supplies for all His lambs and sheep so that we need not worry, fear or panic, regardless of what may threaten to befall us.

Shepherd's pipe. Shepherds frequently carry a reed pipe, or flute, on which they may play either weird or very beautiful music—and they do both. Often while the flock lies resting around the watering place, the shepherd, after eating his meal, takes out his pipe and plays both for his own amusement and for the soothing effect it has on his sheep. He may also sing to himself and to them as he rests in the heat of the day or in the twilight of evening. The sheep "know his voice" (John 10:4), and they enjoy hearing it.

It is easy to imagine David as a lad, singing, reciting poetry and making sweet music as he kept his father's sheep. He became skilled not only with the pipe but also with the harp and probably with other instruments as well. His psalms reflect his musical ability.

Shepherd's cloak. The large, outer cloak worn by shepherds (and others) is a large, flowing, robe-like garment made of heavy, hand-woven wool, either dyed or natural. In North Africa it includes a hood like that of a cape, which is pulled up over the head in wet or cold weather but is permitted to hang down the wearer's back at other times. Often the hood is used as a sort of knapsack in that position. The cloak has short, wide sleeves and, because of its loose-fitting nature, the hands can be withdrawn to the inside for warmth when desired. When night comes, the shepherd pulls the hood over his head, draws in his arms and hands, and curls up his feet inside the warm robe, the garment thus becoming his blanket and bed. This is the reason the Law of Moses prescribed, "If thou at all take thy neighbor's raiment to pledge, thou shalt deliver it unto him by that the sun goeth down: for that is his covering only, it is his raiment for his skin: wherein shall he sleep?" (Ex. 22:26,27).

Since this garment is always large and loose-fitting, there is ample space in the bosom area to carry or to hold a newborn lamb, and often a sick or injured one is carried here while the shepherd is nursing it back to health. The warmth of the shepherd's own body helps to promote healing and health. It was with this in mind that the Prophet Isaiah beautifully portrayed the grace of Jehovah-Messiah in the words, "He shall feed his flock like a shepherd: he shall gather the lambs with his arm, and carry them in his bosom" (Isa. 40:11).

Chapter 10

The Harvest

Grain has long been the principal source of the Palestinian's diet. Therefore, the safe harvesting and preservation of grain is a matter of great consequence to them. No wonder Bible writers often used symbolic language relating to harvesting and harvest time. Almost nothing else would have been more readily understood by the people.

"Fields . . . white already to harvest" (John 4:35). Once the little fields of grain are fully ripened, it is of the utmost concern to the head of the family to reap and preserve the crop immediately, lest some catastrophe befall it. Deep urgency was therefore expressed in the words of Jesus, "The fields . . . are white already to harvest" (v. 35). Once grain is ripe, it must either be harvested or be lost. Often this is also true in relation to spiritual conditions in the world—for example, on certain mission fields.

"Thrust in thy sickle" (Rev. 14:15). Harvesting in Bible times was accomplished meticulously by means of a simple hand sickle. It is still done this way by many people in the Near East and North Africa. This method of harvesting insures that scarcely a spear of grain is missed or spoiled. The reaper cuts the grain and lays it down carefully in handfuls as he proceeds (see Ruth 2:16). Others then follow close behind him and gather these handfuls into larger bundles and bind them as sheaves.

Regarding the use of the sickle, note the following scriptures: Deuteronomy 23:25; Jeremiah 50:16; Joel 3:13; Mark 4:29; and Revelation 14:14-20. The spiritual application is seen in Psalm 126:5,6; Luke 10:2; and John 4:34,35.

Just as the use of the sickle implies the actual cutting of the grain by a person, so the winning of men to Christ is an individual matter. Souls are won to Christ personally and individually by believers. Any Christian can be a soul winner, a spiritual reaper. Some who are particularly gifted and called as "evangelists" have the privilege of winning souls in groups, but the majority are won on an individual basis. Regardless of how they are won—or by whom—each soul that is brought to the Saviour is received by Him as an individual: "He calleth His own sheep by name" (John 10:3).

None are saved merely by having certain family relationships or religious connections. Each individual soul must be taken by the hand of the reaper and placed into the sheaf and then into the garner.

Ruth "gleaned in the field after the reapers" (Ruth 2:3). Following the male reapers—those who cut and bind the grain—are the female gleaners. Their job is to pick up any stems or heads of the precious grain that may elude the reapers as they work rapidly to complete the harvest. Ruth the Moabitess was sent by her mother-in-law, Naomi, to glean in the fields of Boaz. The more prosperous farmers were commanded to allow the poor and less fortunate to glean in their fields free of charge. "The gleanings may enable a widow to have enough bread for the winter" (*Palestinian Quarterly*). In the case of Ruth, the reapers hired by Boaz were instructed to leave her some "handfuls on purpose" (Ruth 2:16). In one day she "beat out . . . an ephah of barley" (v. 17). An ephah is about three-fifths of a bushel. "A diligent gleaner can gather more grain than would be her usual pay for a day," wrote a late resident of Syria.

There are opportunities for all Christians to glean as soul winners. Many a humble believer has gleaned converts for his Saviour even where the more "professional" reaper, the evangelist, has labored. Sometimes unusual people are gleaned and gathered for the Saviour as "handfuls on purpose," especially placed there by the Lord of the Harvest for the gleaner.

The safe storing of grain has always been a matter of special concern to the people of these areas. The grain must be safeguarded against moisture, theft and marauding animals. The most secluded and secret places are used.

Generally, pits for storing the grain are dug in the hard earth, with a comparatively small opening at the top for access. The underground chamber itself might be as much as 8 feet in depth and 4 or 5 feet in breadth, with a mouth of only about 25 inches in diameter at the top. The mouth is then boarded over and covered with straw and earth or turf to conceal its location. In these receptacles grain can be safely stored for a year or longer— until the supply is replenished from a new harvest.

Jeremiah the prophet was probably referring to these underground granaries when he said, "Slay us not: for we have treasures in the field, of wheat, and of barley, and of oil, and of honey" (Jer. 41:8).

Sometimes the storage pit is under the floor of the tent or house where the family lives—usually under the women's quarters, where it would be least suspected and least accessible to thieves.

Here, too, is a spiritual lesson. Once souls have been gathered and brought to Christ, they are kept by Him, safe from all danger of being destroyed or snatched away from Him (Job 11:18; Ps. 91:5; 121:4; John 10:28,29; II Tim. 1:12; 4:18; I Pet. 1:5).

Chapter 11

The Threshingfloor

There are many references in the Bible to threshing and the threshingfloor. I suppose one of the most familiar is the statement of John the Baptist: "He that cometh after me is mightier than I, whose shoes I am not worthy to bear: he shall baptize you with the Holy Ghost, and with fire: whose fan is in his hand, and he will throughly purge his floor, and gather his wheat into the garner; but he will burn up the chaff with unquenchable fire" (Matt. 3:11,12). Two other significant passages are "I have winnowed them with a fan in the gates of the land" (Jer. 15:7, ASV) and "The ungodly are not so: but are like the chaff which the wind driveth away" (Ps. 1:4). In the Book of Ruth we have Naomi's statement concerning Boaz: "Behold, he winnoweth barley to night in the threshingfloor" (3:2).

William M. Thomson, writing in *The Land and the Book*, described a typical eastern threshingfloor: "The construction of the floor is very simple. A circular space from 30 to 50 feet in diameter is made level, if not naturally so, and the ground is smoothed off and beaten solid that the earth may not mingle with the grain in the threshing. In time the floors, especially on the mountains, are covered with a tough, hard, grassy surface, the prettiest and often the only green plot about the village, and there the traveller delights to pitch his tent."

When possible, the top of a flat rock is used, and this is preferable because it is free from mouse and mole holes and ants' nests. It is also cleaner and the mingling of bits of earth with the grain is avoided. The site of Solomon's temple was the site of Araunah's threshingfloor (II Sam. 24:18-25). This rock is under the dome of the Mosque of Omar in Jerusalem, called "The Dome of the Rock." It is almost certain that it was on this same flat rock that Abraham built his altar and prepared to offer Isaac in sacrifice to God.

On the threshingfloor the grain is beaten out of the heads of the stalks and then winnowed and sifted. Threshing is done in one of three ways: with a flail, by the treading of animals, or by the use of a drag.

A flail consists of a wooden bar, or swingle, hinged or tied to a long handle that is swung by the thresher to beat the grain on the floor. We are told that Ruth "beat out that she had gleaned: and it was about an ephah of barley" (Ruth 2:17). Apparently she used some kind of flail. Likewise, we are told that Gideon "was beating out wheat in the winepress, to hide it from the Midianites" (Judg. 6:11, ASV).

Grain is also threshed by having animals walk on the grain on the threshingfloor, literally "treading out the grain." Oxen are commonly used for this purpose. As several of them are driven in a circle or across the floor, successive layers of grain are placed under their feet. The hooves of the animals do the work of threshing. This throws light on the expression "Thou shalt not muzzle the ox when he treadeth out the corn" (Deut. 25:4). The oxen used for treading out the grain were entitled to eat a bit as they did their work. The Apostle Paul quoted this from the Law of Moses to enforce his affirmation, "The labourer is worthy of his reward" (I Tim. 5:18).

The common method of threshing in the Near East is with a drag, or sledge. It is made of heavy, wooden planks and resembles the old-fashioned American "stone boat." Sharp stones or pieces of flint are wedged into holes in the bottom, and these shred the straw to bits as the drag is drawn over it by animals. Drags sometimes have wooden rollers underneath with sharp stones or spikes in them.

Winnowing is accomplished by tossing the grain into the air when there is a fairly brisk breeze, letting the wind blow away the dust and chaff, while the grain falls back to the floor. The instrument used in this process is described in our English Bible as "the fan." However, the word "fan" is misleading. Actually, it is a huge, wooden fork with bent prongs or tines. Because there is generally a breeze blowing in the evening, this is the time when winnowing is usually done. Naomi said, "Behold, [Boaz] winnoweth barley to night in the threshingfloor" (Ruth 3:2).

Because the grain is heaviest, it naturally falls to the floor, while the bulky straw is blown aside. The lighter chaff and dust are carried away and scattered by the wind. In Psalm 1 the ungodly are described as being "like the chaff which the wind driveth away" (v. 4). Sometimes the bulk of the straw and chaff are simply burned with fire. This was the symbolism John the Baptist used in describing the judgment that Christ will ultimately mete out (Matt. 3:12). Isaiah said, "The flame consumeth the chaff" (Isa. 5:24).

After the bulk of the straw and chaff have been removed through the winnowing process, the grain—still mixed with some chaff and foreign matter—must go through a process of hand-sifting. This is done by women, who sit cross-legged on the threshingfloor and rhythmically shake the sieve back and forth above or between their knees until the chaff appears on the top, where they can blow it away. Stones and other foreign substances are at the same time removed from the wheat and likewise, the "tares," or weeds. When the sifting process is finally completed, the farmer has pure, clean grain ready for storage in his granary.

Jesus said to Simon Peter, "Simon, Simon, behold, Satan hath desired to have you, that he may sift you as wheat: but I have prayed for thee, that thy faith fail not" (Luke 22:31,32). This meant that Satan was going to give Simon a very severe shaking, but Jesus added, "When thou art converted, strengthen thy brethren" (v. 32). After Peter had gone through the sifting process, he would be pure and genuine and better able to nurture and strengthen his Christian brethren, just as pure wheat strengthens the body.

God Himself sometimes puts us through the sifting process so we might be better able to bless and strengthen others.

Chapter 12

Potters and Pottery

There are many references and allusions in the Bible to pottery and to potters. Consider the occurrences of such terms as "pots," "potsherd(s)," "potters' vessel," "earthen vessel," "waterpot(s)," "bowl(s)," "vessel(s) of clay" and "broken vessel(s)."

In Bible times most of the household vessels were made of clay and were mainly the products of professional potters, who skillfully formed these vessels on their wheels and then fired them in ovens, or kilns. Cooking and serving vessels were protectively glazed before firing.

Large, unglazed pots were used for storing water, and their porous walls were very effective in cooling the water in hot weather through the process of seepage and external evaporation. Interestingly, the familiar "cup of cold water" referred to by Jesus (Matt. 10:42) is still given as common courtesy in the warm Near East, and the water is drawn from similar vessels.

The large amount of pottery in use was natural in Bible times, since such vessels were very inexpensive in comparison to metal or leather vessels and utensils. Clay was abundant and the potter's fee comparatively small.

Pottery was universal in usage, but it was also fragile and subject to breakage. The various vessels needed to be replaced frequently, making the pottery profession a big business in that simple way of life. This accounts for the frequent references to it in the Scriptures.

Today, across North Africa and throughout the Near East, the potter and the pottery merchant still are common figures in every local community. Small donkeys, almost obscured by their heavy loads of pottery of all types and sizes, are amusing sights.

The equipment used by the potter to form his vessels was extremely simple but nevertheless ingenious. The main device was his wheel, or set of wheels. Note in Jeremiah 18 that, when the prophet went down to the potter's house at the command of God, he said, "Behold, he wrought a work on the wheels" (v. 3). The plural of the word is used because the device was really double-wheeled.

These wheels, as used today, are usually constructed of wood. They are solid, heavy, round devices, usually constructed by the potter himself. Each is composed of two wheels in horizontal positions. One is near the ground, at the lower end of a vertical axle, at the potter's foot, and the other is at the top, just a few inches above the level of his workbench or table. The upper wheel turns when the lower one is kicked into motion by the potter's foot. As the wheels are thus spun, the potter takes a lump of clay and puts it in the center of the upper wheel. As it spins, he forms the vessel with his palms and fingers. The thumb and the first two fingers of the right hand are generally used for the formation of the smaller vessels. In the making of larger vessels, both hands are used—one on the inside and the other on the outside, shaping the vessel according to the potter's design and skill.

Clay in the hand of the potter, molded into whatever form he desires, is used in the Scriptures to illustrate man's relation to God. God is the Divine Potter—the Creator and Redeemer—and man is as clay in His skillful and powerful hands (see Jer. 18:5-9; Rom. 9:20,21).

The wheels for the forming of the clay vessels are always attached to a table or workbench so that the potter has space both to his right and to his left as he works. On the bench is his supply of properly kneaded clay, from which he takes chunks, sized according to the kind of pot or vessel he wishes to make. Close at hand stands a dish of water into which he can dip his fingers when necessary to help in the formation of the vessel, particularly in the final smoothing process. At times he may also add a dash of water to the prepared clay before the formation process to give it the exact consistency needed.

Beside him on the table he temporarily places the finished vessels, which dry very slightly before being put into the kiln for firing.

The lack of attractiveness of a potter's work area adds vividness to God's command to Jeremiah to "go down to the potter's house, and there I will cause thee to hear my words" (Jer. 18:2).

Jeremiah, watching the potter at work, as God had commanded him to do, observed, "The vessel that he made of clay was marred in the hand of the potter: so he made it again another vessel, as seemed good to the potter to make it" (v. 4).

This is not an unusual occurrence in the making of clay pottery. A malformation caused by some defect in the clay itself often develops in the vessel's wall as the clay speeds between the potter's fingers or hands. It might be a tiny stone that escaped the workman's attention during the preparation of the clay. Sometimes it is a chip of wood or a piece of straw, or it may be nothing more than a small, hard bit of clay that had not yielded to the dampening and kneading process.

Sometimes when the potter's fingers strike the unyielding substance, his entire vessel collapses, and the beautiful pot or jar being formed suddenly becomes an unshapely mass of ugly clay! In these instances the potter may brush the whole mass off the wheel and discard it, or he may add a bit of water to the mass of clay and carefully work it between his fingers until he finds and removes the unwanted particle. Then he will set his wheel into motion again and remake the vessel according to his design and purpose.

Jeremiah 18:4 conveys a great lesson regarding creation and redemption: made, marred, made again. Man was made by God; this was a direct act of creation. Man was marred by sin; this was due to an unyielding element in his constitution. The Divine Potter undertakes to remake him; this is according to the original design and pattern (II Cor. 5:17; Col. 3:10).

For the most part, pottery is brittle and extremely fragile. A girl going to the well to fetch water for household use may, because of a slip or by carelessly putting it down, have her vessel break into dozens of pieces, causing her to return empty-handed. This common experience is, in fact, the reason behind the expression in Ecclesiastes 12: "The pitcher be broken at the fountain" (v. 6). It refers to the fragility of human life, the heart being likened to a pitcher or vessel.

Only a slight blow will cause a large, shapely pot or jar to be instantly reduced to a worthless, unsightly mass of broken pieces. This symbol is often used in the Bible to describe divine judgment upon men and nations. "Thou shalt break them with a rod of iron; thou shalt dash them in pieces like a potter's vessel" (Ps. 2:9). "Thus saith the Lord of hosts; Even so I will break this people and this city, as one breaketh a potter's vessel, that cannot be made whole again" (Jer. 19:11). "And he shall rule them with a rod of iron; as the vessels of a potter shall they be broken to shivers" (Rev. 2:27).

A potsherd is a piece of broken pottery. These are usually seen in abundance around a potter's bench or near a pottery shop. In fact, they can be seen almost anywhere in the Near East. Sometimes potsherds are of such a size and shape as to be usable for certain purposes, such as for carrying live coals or for dipping water from a well or pool. They are also used as ladles. There is great significance in Isaiah's statement that "he shall break it as the breaking of the potters' vessel that is broken in pieces; he shall not spare: so that there shall not be found in the bursting of it a sherd to take fire from the hearth, or to take water withal out of the pit" (Isa. 30:14). The judgment of God upon His people was to be so severe that there wouldn't be

52

so much as the counterpart of a usable piece of pottery left.

Another significant use of potsherds was as writing tablets. Fred H. Wright wrote: "In ancient times, when parchment was expensive . . . peasants would use fragments of pottery to . . . scratch memoranda of business transactions." Many such pieces have been unearthed in the Near East by archaeologists and are of significant value in throwing light on ancient history. Archaeologists call these "ostraca."

Job "took him a potsherd to scrape himself withal" (Job 2:8). The prophet had been smitten with "sore boils from the sole of his foot unto his crown [head]" (v. 7). He scraped the repulsive matter and the scabs from his sores with a potsherd because the sores were too disgusting to touch.

When Gideon's brave men went out to face the enemy, they were each to carry an earthenware pitcher with a torch inside in one hand and a trumpet in the other. At a given signal the men were to sound a strong blast on their trumpets and immediately break the pitchers so the lights would shine forth. The sound of the trumpets and the sudden appearance of 300 lights in the darkness around them caused the Midianites to flee in disarray. The Apostle Paul reminds us that we, as Christians, have the light of Jesus Christ "in earthen vessels" (II Cor. 4:7). Unless these vessels are broken, the light cannot shine forth.

God uses broken vessels. Out of broken hearts and broken lives the light of Christ's glory and grace shines the most profusely, whereas unbroken lives seldom radiate His glory.

Chapter 13

Oil in Scripture

Oil was a product that had many uses in Bible times and lands, the majority of which are foreign to our concept of "oil."

There are four Hebrew words in the Old Testament for oil, none of them signifying a petroleum product. To interpret Deuteronomy 33:24 as a prophecy about the petroleum resources of the Middle East is a farfetched interpretation and is unsupported in the passage. The word "oil" here is the word used to signify olive oil.

Professor Arthur B. Fowler said, "Oil in the Bible almost always means olive oil, perhaps the only exception being Esther 2:12, where it is the 'oil of myrrh.' " Even the sacred anointing oil, frequently translated "ointment," though it was compounded with a mixture of spices and perfumes, was basically the oil of the olive.

What may appear to have been a purely cosmetic use of oil in Bible times was really more than just that. Oil was used to cleanse and purify the skin from filth and impurities. As a missionary in Morocco, I discovered that I could remove grease and persistent dirt from my hands more readily with olive oil than with almost anything else, and nothing left my hands feeling more pleasant afterward.

The "soap" referred to in Jeremiah 2:22 definitely signifies a mixture of potash and oil, which was doubtless a standard type of soap used in Jeremiah's day.

The statement in Luke 7:46, "My head with oil thou didst not anoint," indicates that such anointing was an act of great courtesy on the part of a host to his guest. It was a gesture of graciousness and signified the fondness of the host for the one whom he thus anointed. This typifies our spiritual anointing by the Holy Spirit.

I shall always remember the prayer of a godly old veteran missionary who prayed in my presence, "O Lord, we thank Thee for the gracious influences of Thy Holy Spirit upon our lives." Many times since hearing that prayer I have thanked God for that gracious influence of His Spirit in the lives of believers. Then I have asked that it might be profuse and abundant in mine.

When we went to North Africa, it seemed unusual to be using olive oil in all food preparations that required shortening. Even pie crusts had to be made using olive oil as the shortening ingredient. Significantly, in recent years various types of cooking oils have become more widely used in Western countries, largely displacing the old-fashioned use of lard and even butter. Of all the types of oil used as a food ingredient, I feel that olive oil is the most healthful.

Not only was oil used in the preparation of foods, it was also used in the actual cooking or frying of foods. One of the delicacies of the Middle East is leavened bread dough fried in deep olive oil.

There was an abundant supply of oil in Canaan, a fact which demonstrated the richness of the land.

Throughout the Scriptures, oil is symbolic of divine resources, especially as these relate to the Holy Spirit. Christ is the Bread of Life and the Living Water, but it is only as the Holy Spirit reveals Him that the hunger of the soul is satisfied. The honey and the meat of the Word must be mixed with faith and wrought by the Spirit in order to profit those who hear it (Heb. 4:2). It is the Holy Spirit alone who serves the food of the divine Word to our minds and hearts.

Jesus alluded to the use of oil for medicinal purposes in His parable of the Good Samaritan. When this man of compassion saw the victim of the robbers lying by the roadside, he "went to him, and bound up his wounds, pouring in oil and wine" (Luke 10:34). Shepherds habitually used oil to anoint the wounds and bruises which sheep acquired.

References to the use of oil as a cosmetic are fairly frequent in Scripture. Note such passages as II Chronicles 28:15 and Luke 7:46. The word for "oil" is sometimes translated "ointment" in the Old Testament, signifying a perfumed and spiced oil. In Psalm 104:15 we read about oil's making the face shine, a significant reference to the use of oil as a cosmetic.

Oil was apparently used for various cosmetic purposes: to produce fragrance, to cause the skin to "glow" and to soften it. Often after bathing, people would massage their entire bodies with olive oil for both health and cosmetic reasons.

The symbolic meaning of this use is clear. The Holy Spirit brings fragrance and radiance into the life of the man who allows Him to fill and use his life. There is a glow and a spiritual fragrance about the life of a person who is Spirit filled that is unlike anything found in natural man. The beauty of divine holiness ought to be radiated from all Christians. It is always seen in the lives of those who are truly controlled by the Spirit.

A very necessary and notable use of oil in Bible lands was as a fuel for lamps. Lamps were the prime source of light in dwelling places, as well as in the tabernacle and temple. Ordinary lamps were little clay vessels so constructed that a wick lying in the oil and supported at one end in a sort of spout or trough consumed the oil and gave off light. More sophisticated lamps for wealthier homes and for use in the tabernacle and the temple were made of brass and were highly ornamental, yet the basic principle was the same.

The symbolic lesson is quite obvious. The Holy Spirit sets the Christian's heart aflame with divine truth and love. Then He supplies all that is necessary to keep that flame alive in the life. Only as He is permitted to burn within us can any true light be diffused from our lives to the dark world around us (Prov. 4:18). He alone can supply the illumination we need for ourselves and for directing the fect of others to Christ (John 14:6).

Perhaps the most significant use of oil in the Bible was in the anointing of notable men to specific high offices. Priests (Ex. 28:41; 29:7), prophets (I Kings 19:16) and kings (I Sam. 10:1; 16:12,13; I Kings 1:39) were anointed before they began their sacred tasks.

Men chosen of God and appointed to these offices required the wisdom, guidance and power of God to equip them for the discharge of their duties. They were anointed with oil to symbolize the fact that they had already been chosen and anointed by the Spirit of the Lord for their work.

The word "Messiah" means literally "anointed one," and it was this title that indicated the fact that Jesus Christ was anointed by the Spirit for His earthly, redemptive ministry. He combines in Himself all the offices and functions of prophet, priest and king. He is greater than any of the priests of the Aaronic priesthood and greater than all the Old Testament prophets. He is the "King of kings, and Lord of lords" (Rev. 19:16). At the time of His baptism His special anointing by the Holy Spirit for His public ministry was further indicated by the appearance of a heavenly dove and the voice of the Father speaking from heaven.

Christians also have the divine anointing or unction of the Holy Spirit upon them. The unction referred to by the Apostle John (I John 2:20,27) is a general unction, which all believers have. This gives them spiritual understanding and knowledge.

There are also special anointings which the Spirit gives for special tasks to be performed in the service of the Lord. The Christian needs this sort of unction when he witnesses to a lost soul, the preacher needs it when he steps into the pulpit, and the missionary needs it when he presents Christ to the heathen.

Chapter 14

City Gates

In the Old Testament alone the words "gate" or "gates" appear about 400 times. The words have slightly different connotations in different usages. Sometimes reference is made to the entrance or gateway to a city (many of which were protectively walled), sometimes to the actual doors of the gate, and sometimes to the area of the gateway just inside the city wall. This area was usually the popular place of thoroughfare and of the social and civil life of the inhabitants.

In biblical times cities were walled for protection against the attacks and invasions of enemies. The walls were built of brick, stone or dried mud. The thickness and height varied, depending on the existing danger and the ability and resources of the city's ruler or government. I once lived in a city in North Africa whose walls were about 20 to 25 feet in height and 6 to 8 feet in thickness. With such walls surrounding a city, great attention had to be given to providing adequate and secure gates for entry and exit. When danger threatened, these gates were closed and secured at sundown and were not opened until dawn.

The gate sections of the city walls were essentially watchtowers, as well as entryways, and they were considerably greater in height than the sections of wall between them. The gates were actually towers embracing two walls and two sets of doorways—an outer wall with its huge doors as well as an inner one with its own set of doors. This construction is indicated in II Samuel 18:24,25, where we read: "David sat between the two gates: and the watchman went up to the roof over the gate unto [the top of] the wall, and lifted up his eyes, and looked, and behold a man running alone. And the watchman cried, and told the king." Note also verse 33.

The gateway was actually a room within the wall, with both inner and outer gates in the form of heavy swinging doors. Therefore, if an enemy could elude the watchmen and soldiers on the tower above and succeed in battering through the huge outer door, there still remained a second one that had to be broken through before entrance could be achieved into the city.

The gates of these cities were usually ornate and beautiful and were quite often associated with the "glory" of a city. In this connection note Psalm 24:9; 87:2; and Revelation 21:21.

The actual gateway opening was in the form of a gracefully contoured arch. Beside and above the arch were panels of beautiful mosaic work done in a variety of attractive colors. The swinging doors were usually made of thick, heavy wood such as cedar, cypress or even acacia. As a rule, these were beautifully carved and brilliantly painted in a variety of colors. Sometimes they were overlaid with decorative bronze plating for greater strength and protection against fire. This explains the biblical expression "gates of brass" (Ps. 107:16; Isa. 45:2). Attacking armies might shoot burning darts at the city gates, and if the outside gates were constructed only of wood, they would catch fire.

The huge doors, always hung in pairs arranged to swing inward, turned on great stone fittings. These are the "hinges" referred to in Proverbs 26:14. These gigantic doors were so constructed that strong wooden or metal bars could be fitted into clamps on the inside to firmly unite the two and securely "lock" them shut for protection each night or whenever there was a threat of enemy attack. Since the gates were invariably the places of attack upon a city (Ezek. 21:15,22), to "possess the gate" (Gen. 24:60) meant to possess the city.

Immediately inside the city gate there were often beautiful cloisters. These extended along the inside wall in both directions from the exit, and here various civic activities were carried on. The area in front of the gate, inside the wall, provided a large place for public assembly and/or the marketing of food and other merchandise.

Therefore, in addition to the gates of biblical cities being associated with security and protection, they were related to all sorts of public affairs and legal and civil transactions. Even field and farm laborers commonly lodged in the city, and since the men passed through the gate every day, it became a natural meeting place (Ruth 4:1; II Sam. 15:2).

The city gate was also the obvious place to hold large assemblies. For example, in I Kings 22:10 we are told that the kings of Israel and of Judah sat on specially erected thrones "in a void place [empty area] in the entrance of the gate [inside the gate] of Samaria; and all the prophets prophesied before them." Note also Nehemiah 8:1-3: "All the people gathered themselves together as one man into the street [literally, wide place] that was before the water gate. . . . And Ezra the priest brought the law before the congregation. . . . And he read therein before the street [wide place] that was before [inside] the water gate."

In this open area, markets were held (II Kings 7:1; Neh. 3:1,3,28), tribunals were conducted (Deut. 16:18; 21:19), prophets and teachers proclaimed their messages (Prov. 1:21; 8:3; 31:31; Jer. 17:19), and the riffraff of the town gathered (Ps. 69:12). Scribes were also available in their alcove offices along the wall to read and write important or legal documents for those who were unable to do this for themselves. This practice is still common in Near Eastern lands.

Since so many important assemblages and activities were conducted "in the gates" of a city, a seat among the elders in the gates was a high honor (Prov. 31:23). "Oppression in the gates" was a synonym for corruption and the miscarriage of justice (Job 31:21; Prov. 22:22). Apparently, it was not uncommon for kings to hold public audiences in the open area immediately inside the gates of their cities (II Sam. 19:8; I Kings 22:10; Jer. 38:7).

Jesus Christ likened Himself to the gate of the kingdom of God, saying, "I am the door: by me if any man enter in, he shall be saved, and shall go in and out, and find pasture" (John 10:9). The word He used here was the same word used for the gate of a city (Acts 3:2). Important truths come vividly to mind from this: The door or gate was the only means of entrance; only through Jesus Christ can men come into the presence of God or enter into His kingdom. As the gate of the city meant security for those on the inside, so Christ, as the door to God's kingdom, assures the security of all those who come through Him.

Christ further said the gates of hades would not be able to prevail against His Church (Matt. 16:18). In Judges 5:8 there is an indication that the militia commonly assembled in "the gates" of the cities. The gates of a city, especially a capital city, were symbolic of the nation's strength and military prowess. Jesus obviously meant that Satan and all the armies of hell's gates would not be able to conquer His true Church.

Chapter 15

Phylacteries and Garment Borders

Jesus Christ, in His many indictments and woes against the hypocritical Pharisees of His time, made this charge: "But all their works do they for to be seen of men: they make broad their phylacteries, and enlarge the borders of their garments, and love the uppermost rooms at feasts, and the chief seats in the synagogues, and greetings in the markets, and to be called of men, Rabbi, Rabbi" (Matt. 23:5-7).

The first two charges in this indictment—that they made broad their phylacteries and enlarged the borders of their garments—are not easily understood by the average Gentile person in our country and culture. The statements that follow make it obvious that Jesus was charging the Pharisees with spiritual pride and personal arrogance, but the exact meanings of "phylacteries" and "borders of the garments" remain a mystery to many people.

The word "phylactery" is derived from the Greek word *phulakterion*. The basic verb form of this word means "to watch or to be on guard." After the time of the Babylonian captivity, phylacteries were worn by male Jews at morning prayers and at festivals. They came to be regarded as charms or guards, and they were believed to protect the wearer from harm and danger.

Phylacteries are small, handmade leather cases about one cubic inch in size or slightly larger. Inside these are placed strips of writing material on which four passages of Scripture are inscribed: Exodus 13:1-10; Exodus 13:11-16; Deuteronomy 6:4-9; and Deuteronomy 11:13-22. These little leather boxes are equipped with leather thongs, or straps, which are braided in a specific way. The boxes are bound to the wearer's forehead, between his eyes, as well as to his left arm, near his heart.

The making and wearing of phylacteries began with a literal interpretation of Exodus 13:9,16 and Deuteronomy 6:8; 11:18.

Young Jewish men wear phylacteries for the first time when they come to the age of Bar Mitzvah, 13 years. At that time every male Hebrew child goes through a traditional ceremony, and from that time on he is considered a man in his own right and responsible for himself. It is altogether likely that Jesus went through this ceremony in Jerusalem. It may have been following this occasion that "they found him in the temple, sitting in the midst of the doctors, both hearing them, and asking them questions. And all that heard him were astonished at his understanding and answers" (Luke 2:46,47).

The custom of wearing phylacteries has been associated with considerable superstition on the part of some Jewish people. These little leather cases of Scripture wrapped around the head and arm have much the same place in the lives of some Jews as the various kinds of amulets and charms prepared by pagan priests and witch doctors have in the lives of heathen religionists. The very slightest mistake in the preparation of the phylacteries or in the way they are fastened to the forehead and arm with their straps renders them worthless in the mind of the wearer.

When I lived in North Africa, I saw many a Jewish man, beginning a journey in a dilapidated Moroccan bus operated by a fatalistic Muslim driver, hastily wrap his phylacteries around his head and arm. The assumption was that this would protect him from dangers and accidents on the road. I often observed that whenever a Jewish man found himself in a difficult situation or facing possible danger, the normal thing was to bind on his phylacteries with great care and, at times, with considerable emotion.

Note that Jesus did not actually condemn the Pharisees for the wearing of phylacteries, which must have been very common in His day, but rather for showing off their phylacteries. They wore extra-large phylacteries with no other purpose than that of outward show.

Jesus condemned this hypocrisy. He said, "All their works they do for to be seen of men" (Matt. 23:5). They purposely had their own phylacteries made on an enlarged scale and with extra-wide straps to call attention to what was actually religiosity and feigned righteousness. A reading of Matthew 23 shows that the scribes and Pharisees made a great outward profession and show of religion, but their hearts were corrupt and far from God. It was on this ground that Jesus condemned them for their actions.

Jesus also bluntly rebuked the Pharisees for enlarging the borders of their garments. For a correct understanding of this, we need to go back to Numbers 15:38: "Speak unto the children of Israel, and bid them that they make them fringes in the borders of their garments throughout their generations, and that they put upon the fringe of the borders a ribband of blue." Actually, the fringes to which Jesus referred were the tassels on the outer garments which were commonly worn by the Jews in Jesus' time. Today in most countries these garments have been replaced by the prayer shawl, which has the same distinguishing fringes.

To add emphasis to their profession as strict, religious Jews, the Pharisees wore disproportionately large fringes on their garments. This also indicated a great show of outward piety and religiosity, but it was hypocritical, and Jesus condemned it. He despised hypocrisy, and since it was particularly rife among the scribes and Pharisees, He brought strong indictments against them on account of it. He rebuked them for putting on such a great outward show while inwardly remaining carnal and corrupt.

As Christians, in the light of Jesus' strong denunciation, we must beware of having a mere outward profession with no reality of life behind it. Such hypocritical profession only causes grief and invokes the displeasure of God toward us.

Chapter 16

Coals of Fire on the Head

In Romans 12:20 the Apostle Paul wrote: "If thine enemy hunger, feed him; if he thirst, give him drink: for in so doing thou shalt heap coals of fire on his head."

I would like to suggest what I believe is a better explanation of that verse than the ones usually given. First of all, we must note the implication of the entire context of this statement. Verse 19 admonishes us, "Dearly beloved, avenge not yourselves, but rather give place unto wrath: for it is written, Vengeance is mine; I will repay, saith the Lord." This statement indicates that no act of a Christian toward an adversary should in any sense be motivated by revenge or judgment. Bear this in mind. Verse 21 exhorts, "Be not overcome with evil, but overcome evil with good." This means that a Christian is not to react in any spirit of reprisal or vengeance.

Numerous interpretations have been given to Paul's statement, "In so doing thou shalt heap coals of fire on his head" (v. 20). The most common interpretation is that a Christian's act of kindness will awaken the memory of wrongdoing in his enemy, and this will sting the enemy with penitence and remorse. The implication is that the enemy's pain in some way gratifies the natural instinct of revenge, and this instinct actually becomes an underlying motive for deeds of outward kindness. To me, this interpretation still seems to spell out "vengeance" of some sort. In fact, Dean Henry Alford boldly states: "I understand the words, 'in thus doing, you will be taking the most effectual vengeance,' as effectual as if you had heaped coals of fire on his head." To me, this interpretation simply does not fit the context, nor does it correspond to Christian ethics. Consider these statements: "Dearly beloved, avenge not yourselves" and "Vengeance is mine; I will repay, saith the Lord" (v. 19).

Another interpretation suggested by an eminent commentator is that the apostle's metaphor alludes to those who melted metals as refiners, not only by putting fire under the metals but also heaping it over them for maximum heat. They believe the meaning is "to melt your adversary into repentance and friendship." In other words, you will win a friend by heaping coals of warmth and kindness upon him. To me this seems farfetched and becomes a strained interpretation of what the apostle obviously intended as a simple and understandable statement.

Some believe the words "heap coals of fire on his head" refer to the glow and burn of shame which would accompany the receiving of benefits from an enemy, even in the case of a very profane person. It would leave within him a burning sense of guilt. The enemy would feel deep shame and remorse as a result of the Christian's kindnesses, like coals of fire burning upon his head. The sense would be that of a burning inner conscience. But neither does this, in my judgment, explain the true meaning of the apostle's exhortation.

Here is what I believe to be the most natural and obvious interpretation of the apostle's statement. In Bible times, and even today in Bible lands, the only fire the people have in their dwellings is kept in a brazier or in a clay pot. Here, coals of charcoal are continuously kept burning. If this charcoal fire ever goes out, some member of the family must take the brazier or pot to a neighbor's house to borrow some live coals from him. In those countries almost everything is carried on the head—water jars, baskets of fruit, vegetables, or any other article, including the fire-pot. After receiving some fresh coals from her neighbor, a female member of the family lifts the brazier to her head and starts for home. If the neighbor happens to be a truly generous woman, she will "heap" the brazier or pot with fresh, hot coals; if she is stingy or reluctant, she may only give a few tiny embers.

I therefore think that when the Apostle Paul exhorted Christians to feed an enemy and to give him drink, he was saying that this would be like heaping his empty, cold brazier with live coals for his food and warmth. This would be a symbol of the finest generosity and sincerity. This meaning of the apostle's words certainly fits the whole context.

Not all will accept this interpretation, but to me it seems the most logical and satisfying. I submit it to you for earnest consideration. Above all, as Christians, let us always practice kindness in dealing with all people, friend and foe alike.

70

Chapter 17

Much Ado About a Small Coin

"What woman having ten pieces of silver, if she lose one piece, doth not light a candle, and sweep the house, and seek diligently till she find it? And when she hath found it, she calleth her friends and her neighbours together, saying, Rejoice with me; for I have found the piece which I had lost. Likewise, I say unto you, there is joy in the presence of the angels of God over one sinner that repenteth" (Luke 15:8-10).

Have you ever wondered why a woman would be so emotional over a tiny coin, worth about 15 cents? What would cause her to clean her house from top to bottom to find something of so little value? And even more strangely, what would cause her to gather her neighbors and friends together for a "celebration" after she had found the tiny piece of silver? Does this not seem to be somewhat incongruous?

Most peculiar of all, why would Jesus compare such excitement and celebration to that which exists in heaven when a lost sinner comes into God's family through repentance and confession? And why would He use the parable of this lost coin on the same level and for the same purpose as that

71

of a lost sheep being sought and found or of a lost son coming home?

To the uninitiated mind in the Western culture, this seems to be a rather strange parable. If a housewife in our culture should lose a dime, she certainly would not make such a fuss over it as all this. What then is the true significance of the parable? In order to discover this, we must ask, What is the background of the scene Jesus used as an illustration?

To rightly understand, we must be familiar with the traditional custom and value of a wife's coins. A practice of long standing in Bible lands, still followed in some places, is that when a woman marries, her bridegroom gives her a wedding gift of a string of ten pieces of silver. These she prizes very highly and guards very carefully. The string of silver coins is often worn on her headdress, or it might be worn around her neck.

In North Africa, Bible traditions and customs are still commonly observed. It is the custom, particularly among the country women, for the wife to wear her wealth in the form of jewelry made up of silver or gold coins. Naturally, the loss of any of these would be considered a calamity.

In Bible times it was a particularly great calamity if a wife lost one of the coins which her husband had given her at the time of their wedding, because such carelessness on her part would be regarded by her husband as a lack of affection and respect for him. He might even suspect her of having spent the coin for some secret, sinister purpose. One writer who has had considerable contact with the Holy Land suggests that her husband might even think she had purchased the favors of a secret lover with the missing money, and he could therefore divorce her on account of it. While this seems a bit farfetched, I cannot say it is outside the realm of possibility.

Among the Jewish people, the "nuptial coins" worn by the wife were held to be very sacred and could not be taken by a creditor to pay a debt. The wife could use this money only in the case of destitution in widowhood.

With this background in mind as we read the parable, we can understand the concern and anxiety a woman would have if she lost one of her coins and why she called her neighbors together for a celebration when she found it. This gives real force to the parable the Lord used, and no doubt the illustration made a deep impression on the minds of His listeners. One can also see that this parable is just as important as the other two in Luke 15 in illustrating the joy that exists in the presence of the angels of God over one sinner that repents and comes into the Father's house.

Chapter 18

Whited Sepulchers

When Jesus was verbally scourging the scribes and Pharisees of His day for their hypocrisy, He told them, "Woe unto you, scribes and Pharisees, hypocrites! for ye are like unto whited sepulchres, which indeed appear beautiful outward, but are within full of dead men's bones, and of all uncleanness. Even so ye also outwardly appear righteous unto men, but within ye are full of hypocrisy and iniquity. Woe unto you. . . . Ye build the tombs of the prophets, and garnish the sepulchres of the righteous, and say, If we had been in the days of our fathers, we would not have been partakers with them in the blood of the prophets. Wherefore ye be witnesses unto yourselves, that ye are the children of them which killed the prophets. Fill ye up then the measure of your fathers. Ye serpents, ye generation of vipers, how can ye escape the damnation of hell?" (Matt. 23:27-33).

Though the meaning of Jesus' words here would likely be obvious to any Bible reader, a specific knowledge of graves and sepulchers of that land and day should serve to make His indictment more vivid and potent.

74

Even when a body was buried in an ordinary grave in the ground, a fairly prominent tomb of mortar was promptly erected over the site. Some, of course, were more elaborate than others, depending on the prominence of the person buried and on the affluence of the surviving family. But rich or poor, all the tombs were invariably kept white by frequent reapplications of freshly slaked lime whitewash. The tombs were thus constantly kept snow white and spotless. The careful rewhite-washing of all the graves in the burial grounds was a routine activity prior to special civic or religious holidays or feasts. This is still the practice in the countries of the Middle East. The process may be repeated several times annually.

Actually, these cemeteries, particularly from a little distance, give the appearance of great beauty and attractiveness. The burial grounds are often whiter and cleaner looking than the homes of the people.

The outward whiteness of the tombs Jesus was referring to, giving the impression of purity and cleanness, was utterly in contrast to the contents of the grave itself, where there was only stench, putrefaction and corruption. Perhaps there is nothing more revolting to a human being than to look into an open tomb containing a partially decayed human body. The sight and the stench are nauseating. And this was particularly true for the people of Jesus' day, because for them even to touch or come into contact with a dead body or anything that pertained to it meant to be ceremonially defiled.

No matter how frequently the tombs were whitewashed on the outside, they still contained only corruption on the inside—decayed or decaying bodies and bones. Though the tombs had been made to appear attractive on the outside, the whitewash had made no difference on the inside.

Jesus' figure of speech must have conveyed a very strong message to the people to whom He spoke. Perhaps no symbol of hypocrisy could have been stronger than that of graves outwardly whitewashed and spotlessly clean but full of corruption within. This was exactly the way Jesus looked upon the scribes and Pharisees, and, therefore, this was the way He described them. He insisted that man's religion was not to be merely an outward declaration for special occasions, such as religious feasts, but it was to be a life principle of inward purity and outward testimony.

Let us remember that God still looks at hypocrisy in exactly the same way, no matter where He sees it—even in our own lives. Our inward state must correspond to our outward show. God hates and decries man's hypocrisy.

Chapter 19

Water and Irrigation

Some of the significance and force of the original languages of the Bible is lost to English readers due to the fact that the same word is often used in our English versions to translate several Hebrew or Greek words of varied meanings. The converse is likewise true: the same original word may be translated by several English words in our Bibles.

A case in point, and a significant one, is in the very familiar Psalm 1. We read here that the man of God who separates himself from evil companions and surroundings and constantly meditates in the law of the Lord "shall be like a tree planted by the rivers of water, that bringeth forth his fruit in his season" (v. 3). While the basic meaning of the original is still apparent in this translation, some of its actual force and beauty has been lost. I was first impressed by this when I read the psalm for the first time in the Arabic-language Bible. To my surprise, I noted that in the Arabic it does not read, "like a tree planted by the *rivers of water*"; rather, it reads, "like a tree planted by the *irrigation ditches.*"

A check with the Hebrew text shows that the Arabic version is correct. The word in the Hebrew is *peleg*, which does not really signify "rivers" but rather "irrigation ditches." Young's concordance gives the meaning of the word as "an artificial water course," that is, not a naturally flowing stream of water but a man-made one. The word appears ten times in the Old Testament of the King James Version; nine times it is translated "river."

In one instance it is translated "streams." This is in Psalm 46:4: "There is a river, the *streams* whereof shall make glad the city of God." Here the language is symbolic, for no such river ever flowed through Jerusalem. The picture drawn here is a very striking one: a major river is flowing through a population center, and from it a series of irrigation canals or "streams" branch out for water distribution.

In the first Psalm the picture is very graphic. Through a surrounding stretch of arid territory flows an irrigation ditch with an unfailing supply of water, and all along this canal are verdant trees flourishing with fruit.

It is always an impressive sight to see an irrigated area in otherwise barren country—a familiar scene in many parts of the world. In places where there are no rivers, and hence no natural supply of water, men dig wells to tap the hidden underground supply and bring it to the surface. There, by means of irrigation ditches, it is distributed to their fields and orchards.

The application is beautiful. The Christian in this world often senses that he is in a dry and thirsty land. His surroundings are often spiritually dry. But he is not dependent on the natural circumstances that surround him; he is nourished by continual meditation in the Word of God. That Word supports, refreshes and nourishes him, just as the irrigation ditch nourishes trees along its banks, even in desert territory. The true man of God, through drawing refreshment and nourishment from God's holy Word, is able to bear fruit even in the most spiritually hopeless surroundings, where sin and evil may abound.

What is the basic difference between a natural river and an irrigation ditch? Perhaps the contrast can best be indicated by saying the river depends on natural circumstances for its water supply, whereas the irrigation ditch is kept flowing by artificial means. Rivers often depend on heavy snows melting on adjacent mountaintops or on rainfall in distant areas which must reach them through natural channels. If the snow on the mountains is light or the rainfall is sparse, the river will dwindle, and in some instances it may go completely dry. By way of contrast, the irrigation ditch is usually kept supplied with water by means of some kind of pump, powered by men or animals in ancient times and in primitive territories and by gasoline or electric motors in modern places. Huge dams are sometimes constructed in rivers to conserve for irrigation the water supply that would otherwise be completely lost to the area. Thousands of acres of land that would otherwise be desert have thus been made productive in various countries of the world.

God's Word is the supernatural supply of strength and nourishment for His children. The one who meditates constantly in the Word of God will be like a fruit tree planted beside an irrigation ditch. Jesus pointed out to His disciples in John 15 the essential relationship between the bearing of fruit and the abiding of His Word in us.

In Psalm 1:3 we see several clear lessons: The person who lives close to the "irrigation ditch" of God's Word finds a constant supply for his soul. He experiences continual freshness and growth, like a tree planted where it can receive a constant supply of water. He is a fruitful Christian, bringing forth "fruit in his season." He never becomes dry and lifeless: "His leaf also shall not wither." And he will always experience the blessing of God on his life and activities: "Whatsoever he doeth shall prosper."

There is no way to live a fresh, abundant and fruitful Christian life apart from constant reading and meditation in God's Word. Those who are continually immersed in the Word will inevitably grow in Christian experience and constantly bear spiritual fruit.

Accept the challenge! Plant yourself beside the irrigation ditch of God's Word and let your roots feed constantly on the abundant supply of living water. You can live a joyous, useful Christian life through constant contact with the Word of God.

Chapter 20

The 'Sop' of the Last Supper

"When Jesus had thus said, he was troubled in spirit, and testified, and said, Verily, verily, I say unto you, that one of you shall betray me. Then the disciples looked one on another, doubting of whom he spake. Now there was leaning on Jesus' bosom one of his disciples, whom Jesus loved. Simon Peter therefore beckoned to him, that he should ask who it should be of whom he spake. He then lying on Jesus' breast saith unto him, Lord, who is it? Jesus answered, He it is, to whom I shall give a sop, when I have dipped it. And when he had dipped the sop, he gave it to Judas Iscariot, the son of Simon. And after the sop Satan entered into him" (John 13:21-27).

This passage of Scripture raises a number of perplexing questions to the average Bible reader. How could the disciple John "lean on Jesus' bosom" while eating a meal? How could one man possibly be "lying on the breast" of another in the course of dining? What was the "sop" to which Jesus referred? And what is the meaning of "when he had dipped the sop, he gave it to Judas"?

To understand the scene, one must remember that oriental furnishings and customs are very different from ours. Chairs and tables like we use are not traditional oriental fixtures. Country people, who are often tent dwellers, along with the poorer class of city residents usually sit cross-legged in a circle around a low table. They sit on rugs or straw mats with their feet covered by their flowing robes.

The only dishes on the table are those containing the food; separate dishes are not provided for each person eating the meal. One large dish of food is customarily placed on the table at a time, and all dip into that dish and eat from it. Such utensils as knives, forks and spoons are absent; these are, in fact, comparatively recent innovations and are peculiar to Western civilization.

In city homes and among the more affluent in rural areas, people lounge on divans which circle the table. But the food is still served in one large tray or dish, and all dip into it in common. To eat with an Easterner implies a much closer bond of friendship than it connotes in our Western culture.

In affluent circles or at times of special religious or civil ceremony, a triclinium table might be used. This is a table with combined couches around three sides, the table itself being U-shaped so that food can be served from the open center. Each guest eats while reclining on a couch, with the upper part of the body resting on the left arm, the head raised, and the legs and feet stretched out behind him. Cushions are always provided, to be placed behind the back for added comfort. With all diners in this same position, it means that the head of the second guest is opposite the breast of the first, so that if he desires to speak secretly to him he may simply lean back on his breast and speak in

82

a whisper. Or, as a token of affection, one may actually rest his head on the other's bosom—not an uncommon act in the East.

This was evidently the arrangement made for the Last Supper, which Jesus ate with His disciples. This clarifies at once the significance of Simon Peter's beckoning to John "that he should ask who it should be of whom he [Jesus] spake" (v. 24) when He said, "One of you shall betray me" (v. 21). In response, John, leaning on Jesus' breast, quietly asked Him, "Lord, who is it?" (v. 25). Jesus, in turn, quietly said to John, "He it is, to whom I shall give a sop, when I have dipped it" (v. 26). John could then whisper the answer to the one next to him, and so on, until the message got to Simon, with Judas being completely unaware of this part of the conversation.

This posture while eating also makes clear how the events referred to in Luke 7:38 and John 12:3 could occur. The Luke account speaks of a woman of the city, who came into the house where Jesus was dining, "stood at his feet behind him weeping, and began to wash his feet with tears, and did wipe them with the hairs of her head, and kissed his feet, and anointed them with the ointment." Since Jesus was reclining on a raised divan, with His feet away from the table, the woman could simply bend over His feet and do this.

Now let us clarify the manner in which Judas was identified as the Lord's betrayer at the Last Supper. When Jesus said, "He that dippeth his hand with me in the dish, the same shall betray me" (Matt. 26:23), He was simply asserting that one of the disciples then eating with Him would be the betrayer, not identifying which one it would be. They were all in the process of eating out of the same dish when He spoke the words, "It is one of the twelve, that dippeth with me in the dish" (Mark 14:20).

But in John's Gospel notice the words that Jesus whispered to John, who was resting his head on His breast: "He it is, to whom I shall give a sop, when I have dipped it" (13:26). This was the act to mark the betrayer. What was the "sop" Jesus referred to? Since they did not use silverware in their eating, it was quite natural to break off little pieces of bread to dip up food from the dish. By this means they conveyed the food to the mouth. The piece of bread was used as a kind of spoon or scoop to pick up solid portions of food and to sop up liquids or broths. It has been my experience that bread is eaten with everything, at all stages of the meal, to facilitate the handling of the other food. One soon learns to use bits of bread in place of a fork or spoon. It was that bit of bread, dipped into the dish, that is referred to as the "sop" in the Scriptures.

Quite common in the Near East, it is an act of courtesy on the part of the host to dip a bit of bread in a dish, pick up a choice morsel of food and put it into the mouth of his guest. So Jesus' gesture to Judas was not particularly extraordinary; but it does indicate that even though He knew the actions Judas was then contemplating, He extended to him an act of courteous friendship and love. One writer, Abraham Rihbany, described this act of the Lord as sign language, by which He was saying, "Judas, My disciple, I have infinite pity for you. You have proved false, you have forsaken Me in your heart; but I will not treat you as an enemy, for I have not come to destroy, but to fulfill. Here is My sop of friendship, and 'that thou doest do quickly.' " The sop He gave to Judas was the highest expression of love He could show him and was doubtless His last attempt to call Judas to a sense of the horrible sin he was then planning to commit. Was this not a real token of infinite love?

Chapter 21

Foot Washing

In John 13 we read the moving account of Jesus' washing the feet of His disciples. During the Last Supper, Jesus got up from the table, laid aside His outer garments and tied a towel around Himself. Then, pouring water into a basin, He stooped down to wash the disciples' feet. With this act of self-humiliation complete, He said to His disciples, "If I then, your Lord and Master, have washed your feet; ye also ought to wash one another's feet. For I have given you an example, that ye should do as I have done to you" (vv. 14,15).

Some Christians have understood from this that foot washing should be practiced in the church as an ordinance much like the Lord's Supper and baptism. There is evidence that Ambrose, the bishop of Milan, practiced this in his church in the latter part of the fourth century. Augustine, though he did not positively sponsor the practice, did intimate that to do this would be a commendable act of humility. Certain religious denominations and groups practice literal foot washing to this day.

The godly old commentator Matthew Henry wrote: "(1.) Some have understood this literally. ... (2.) But doubtless it is to be understood figuratively.... Three things our Master hereby designed to teach us:—[1.] A humble condescension.... Christ had often taught his disciples humility, and they had forgotten the lesson; but now he teaches them in such a way as surely they could never forget. [2.] A condescension to be serviceable. To wash one another's feet is to stoop to the meanest office of love, for the real good and benefit one of another.... [3.] A serviceableness to the sanctification one of another: *Ye ought to wash one another's feet*, from the pollutions of sin.... We cannot satisfy for one another's sins, ... but we may help to purify one another from sin.... We must sorrow for the failings and follies of our brethren, ... must wash our brethren's polluted feet in tears."

My own experiences in a land where the practices and customs of Bible times have been perpetuated lead me to agree with this view, though not in any way indicting or disparaging those who feel otherwise.

In the countries we call "Bible lands," the majority of the people wore only sandals, and their feet readily became soiled. Most roads were not hard-surfaced, and in the rainy season they became extremely muddy and unsanitary.

Because the feet became dirty so easily, it was customary for a man entering a home to remove his sandals in the vestibule and wash his feet before proceeding into the house. The homes of men who were affluent enough to have several servants always had a particular servant at the door assigned to the task of washing the feet of all who entered, particularly guests. The *Zondervan Pictorial Bible Dictionary*, edited by Merrill C. Tenney, states that when a visitor enters a house, the lowest servant is detailed to wash his feet. This I can personally verify. The washing of feet was the least desirable of all the tasks of servitude and was considered to be extremely humiliating.

The relationship between the guest and the servant at the time of foot washing was vividly demonstrated to me on one occasion when I was visiting the house of a district chieftain in Morocco. We had been preaching in a nearby marketplace, which had turned to a sea of mud because of heavy rains. When we arrived at the chieftain's home, a servant was dispatched to wash our feet at the entrance. It is always humiliating for a servant to be assigned to wash a guest's feet, but for a proud Muslim to have to wash the feet of a despised Christian was doubly humiliating and irritating. If looks could have killed, we would have had clean feet on dead bodies!

The foot washing of John 13 occurred at the time of the Passover, when the spring rains were falling. The streets of Jerusalem were no doubt particularly muddy and unclean at the time. Obviously, the disciples should not have come to the Passover table with unwashed feet, but apparently they did. While sharing the Last Supper with them, Jesus insisted that their feet be clean. Apparently not one of the disciples had volunteered to wash the feet of the others; therefore, the Lord Jesus stooped to this most humiliating of all tasks and washed their feet Himself.

When He had washed their feet, He said. in essence, "As I have stooped to render to you the lowliest and most humiliating of all services, so ought you to be prepared to render to one another the lowliest and humblest service." The Jamieson, Fausset, and Brown commentary says that the words, "ought to wash one another's feet," should be taken, "not in the narrow sense of a literal washing, profanely caricatured by Popes and Emperors, but by the very humblest *real* services one to another."

That this is the correct understanding is indicated by the words of Jesus in verse 7: "What I do thou knowest not now; but thou shalt know hereafter." If literal foot washing had been meant, such words would have been pointless. He also said, "If I wash thee not, thou hast no part with me" (v. 8). Surely this could not apply to the literal washing of physical feet. Jesus went on to say, "He that is washed needeth not save to wash his feet, but is clean every whit" (v. 10). He must have been referring to spiritual cleansing rather than to physical washing.

Matthew Henry aptly wrote: "The transaction was very solemn, . . . and four reasons are here intimated why Christ did this:—1. That he might testify his love to his disciples, *v.* 1,2. 2. That he might give an instance of his own voluntary humility and condescension, *v.* 3-5. 3. That he might signify to them spiritual washing, which is referred to in his discourse with Peter, *v.* 6-11. 4. That he might set them an example, *v.* 12-17."

Chapter 22

Tears and Tear Bottles

Tears are mentioned frequently in the Bible. The tear bottle is mentioned only once, though perhaps it is alluded to in a number of other passages.

In Psalm 56 David prays, "Put thou my tears into thy bottle" (v. 8). The heading of this psalm indicates that it is a prayer of David, commemorating the time when he fled from King Saul and had been captured by his nation's worst enemy, the Philistines. He had already been anointed king of Israel but had not yet ascended to the throne. The experience out of which this psalm grew was difficult for David, and his prayers—and tears— were numerous.

Notice the intensity of David's desperation, expressed in these words: "Man would swallow me up; he . . . oppresseth me. Many . . . fight against me. Every day they wrest my words. They mark my steps, when they wait for my soul" (vv. 1,2,5,6). He cried to God in this difficult time, and his prayer was accompanied by tears. Such experiences are not uncommon to God's people today. The Christian's prayers can bring tears— actual tears as well as inner tears of agony.

Sorrow, suffering and tears are results of sin. After man first sinned in the Garden of Eden, God promised to both Adam and Eve that sorrow would be a part of human life. To Eve He said, "In sorrow thou shalt bring forth children" (Gen. 3:16). And to Adam He said, "In sorrow shalt thou eat of it [the ground] all the days of thy life" (v. 17).

The expression "Put thou my tears into thy bottle" seems unusual to us. In Persia and in Egypt, tears were wiped from the cheeks and the eyes of the mourner and were stored in a tear bottle, where they were carefully preserved. The custom was probably based on the belief that these tears would prove to God that the person had been righteous during his lifetime and that God would mercifully reward him. That such a belief existed seems to be substantiated by the fact that the individual's tear bottle was buried with him at death. Tear bottles have been found in many of the ancient tombs of Egypt and elsewhere throughout the East. These bottles were made of alabaster, since glass was not yet in use.

During his imprisonment among the Philistines, David did not have a tear bottle of his own. Thus, he asked the Lord to store his tears and to record them in His divine record book. He was praying that God would record his sufferings and sorrows and that He would not forget his tears. One is reminded of God's statement to Moses regarding the sufferings of His people in ancient Egypt: "I have surely seen the affliction of my people . . . and have heard their cry by reason of their taskmasters; for I know their sorrows" (Ex. 3:7). In the preceding chapter we read that Israel's cry "came up unto God. And God heard their groaning" (2:23,24).

The story in Luke 7:36-50 has often puzzled Bible readers. While Jesus ate at Simon's house, a woman "stood at his feet behind him weeping, and began to wash his feet with tears, and did wipe them with the hairs of her head, and kissed his feet, and anointed them with the ointment" (v. 38). How could a woman shed enough tears to wash a person's feet?

It is possible that the woman brought her bottle of tears to Jesus. These tears, saved during her lifetime, were the symbol of her sorrow. She washed Christ's feet with her tears—an act which was meaningful to the woman and also to Jesus. She gave her most precious items—her tears and the box of costly ointment, or perfume—to Christ. Instead of keeping these treasures until she died, this woman poured them out on Jesus as tokens of her love and gratitude for His mercy.

It will be wonderful when "God shall wipe away all tears" (Rev. 21:4) from the eyes of His redeemed people. Then they will live eternally in His presence, where there "shall be no more death, neither sorrow, nor crying, neither shall there be any more pain" (v. 4). Tears and tear bottles will be discarded forever!

Chapter 23

Mirrors

In the King James Version of the Bible several terms are used to denote "mirror" or "mirrors." These references are infrequent but significant: "lookingglasses" (Ex. 38:8); "looking glass" (Job 37:18); "glasses" Isa. 3:23); and "glass" (I Cor. 13:12; II Cor. 3:18; James 1:23,24).

The English translations for the Greek and Hebrew words are misleading because mirrors used in Bible times were not made of glass. Glass mirrors have existed only since the Middle Ages. Those first made in Venice in the 16th century were backed with a thin tin-mercury mixture. Those made after 1840 had a thin silver coating. The introduction of plate glass in the 17th century caused mirrors to become items of household furniture.

In Bible times mirrors were made of metal. Hence "mirror" is used instead of "glass" and words derived from "glass" in almost all versions of the Bible but the King James.

In Exodus 38:8 we read: "He made the laver of brass, . . . of the lookingglasses of the women."

The mirrors used in Bible times were usually made of highly polished bronze ("brass" in the Bible), which reflected any image set in front of it. In Job 37:18 Elihu says the sky resembles a "molten looking glass," comparing the brightness of the sky to highly polished metal.

The manufacturing of mirrors of this type was revived during World War I, when soldiers used them as trench mirrors. Rather than being made of bronze or brass, the mirrors were made of polished, chrome-plated steel.

Naturally, the image reflected by the ancient metal mirrors was not as clear as that of modern glass mirrors. Therefore, the Apostle Paul wrote: "Now we see through a glass, darkly, (I Cor. 13:12), or "For now we see dimly (indistinctly) in a mirror."

The statement in Exodus 38:8 is quite significant. During their long and arduous wilderness experience, the women of Israel gladly gave up even their mirrors for the construction of the tabernacle. A great deal of brass was required for various parts of the tabernacle, especially the large laver, which was formed of solid brass.

To the Jewish women in Exodus, mirrors were as important as they are to women today. To give their mirrors to the Lord's work meant the surrendering of a chief item of personal vanity. Willingness to surrender such an item to the Lord demonstrates the work of God in one's heart.

American men and women spend 18 percent more on personal-care products and services than they spend on all religious and welfare activities.

Many Christians spend much more for cosmetics than they give to world missions. When they stand before the Judgment Seat of Christ to give an account of their lives, as Paul vividly portrays in I Corinthians 3, how will they explain this imbalance?

Chapter 24

Marriage Customs

In the Bible, marriage holds a very prominent and sacred place. In the lands of the Near East, even to the present time, the marriage ceremony is one of the chief events in family and community life.

Marriage is referred to in the Bible in such passages as Psalm 19:5; Isaiah 49:18; 61:10; 62:5; Jeremiah 2:32; Matthew 9:15; and Revelation 21:2,9. Above all else, serious Bible students should remember that the human marriage relationship is used to symbolize the relationship between the Lord and His redeemed people (Eph. 5:21-33). In the Old Testament, Israel, God's ancient people, was pictured as the wife of Jehovah (Hos. 2:14-20); and in the New Testament the Church is called "the bride" of Jesus Christ (John 3:29; Rev. 19:7-9).

In modern life there are many variations in the details of the marriage ceremony, and this was also true in Bible times. Then, as now, customs depended to a great extent on the station in life of the parties being married. Because of this, it is difficult to give a precise, overall description of the marriage ceremony in Bible times and say, "This is the way it was." But we can point out some general facts based on a study of the Bible and the customs observed in Bible lands to the present time.

The formal betrothal usually took place quite a long time before the marriage—sometimes several years before. The family of the bridegroom-elect arranged the betrothal with the parents of the young woman he desired in marriage, and a certain dowry was settled on. Among Jewish people this betrothal cannot even now be broken without a paper of divorce from a rabbi.

The actual marriage ceremony involved several days of festivity and customary rites. The bridal procession to the home of the groom for the consummation of the nuptials was always a gala event, even among the poorer people. While the exact pattern followed in Bible lands at the present time differs among Christians, Jews and Muslims, this was the general procedure. The bride had a trousseau and a variety of household goods. Some of these may have been purchased with the dowry money, and some may have been given as wedding gifts. The gifts were usually borne before her by those making up the procession.

The procession, which usually wound through the streets at night, moved slowly and was preceded by musicians and dancers and sometimes by those performing wild feats of horsemanship. The bride herself may have arrived either riding an animal, being carried in a sedan chair, or perhaps on foot, but in any case she was invariably covered by a colorful canopy. She was usually dressed rather gaily but with her hair flowing loosely. Her coiffure was cared for by some of her maidens-in-

97

waiting after she reached the home of her groom. This procession was made up of both men and women—some from among her own circle of friends and some from her parent's family. When the bride arrived at the home of her husband-to-be, the women of his household and the invited guests met her with songs and censers of burning incense and conducted her into the best room in the house, which was beautifully decorated as the bridal chamber.

The groom himself was absent when the bridal party arrived. He purposely stayed away and spent the time at the home of one of his relatives, where he also ate his supper. He and the party that made up his procession then dressed themselves properly for the occasion and had a good time together before proceeding to his own home where his bride had already been received. After all the expected members of his party were courteously welcomed and their congratulations had been received, they proceeded in the bridegroom's procession to the awaiting bride at the house of the bridegroom. This procession was usually made between 11:00 p.m. and midnight. Flaming torches were held aloft by special bearers and the procession swept slowly along to the groom's house, where the bride's attendants were waiting to meet them.

Great crowds often assembled on the balconies, on the garden walls, and on the flat roofs of the houses on each side of the road to watch the impressive spectacle. The bridegroom was the center of the special interest, and whispering voices were often heard saying, "Look! There he is!" As they traveled along, women raised their voices in a special shrill cry which expressed joy at marriages and at other times of family and public rejoicing. As the procession approached the bridegroom's own house, the pace was quickened and the cry was raised with louder voices: "He is coming, he is coming!" Just prior to his arrival, the bride's maidens-in-waiting came out a short distance with lamps and candles to meet the procession and to light up the entrance as the groom's party approached the house.

Once the bride and the groom were together in his home, they were seated together under a brilliantly decorated canopy, and although there were no special marriage vows in our occidental sense of the term, the nuptials were culminated in a festival of great pomp. This was given by the father of the groom rather than by the father of the bride. This feast usually lasted from three to seven days, the festivities on the last day being the most elaborate and elegant.

Residents of Bible lands have remarked that in some weddings, when the bridegroom's party entered his house to celebrate the marriage, the doors were promptly closed and no others were allowed to enter thereafter. Also, in some instances the groom's household provided special wedding garments for all guests, and these had to be worn. Such customs, of course, throw much light on the parables of the Bible, such as that which tells of a king who gave a marriage celebration for his son (Matt. 22) and the parable of the ten virgins (ch. 25).

Chapter 25

Razors and Shaving

The assumption of Bible writers seems to have been that everyone knew that all men normally had beards. To have the hair of one's beard plucked out or shaved off was a mark of shame and humiliation. "There came certain from Shechem, from Shiloh, and from Samaria, even fourscore men, having their beards shaven, and their clothes rent, and having cut themselves" (Jer. 41:5). Isaiah, in predicting the judgment of God on Moab and its cities, said, "On all their heads shall be baldness, and every beard cut off" (Isa. 15:2). The "baldness" referred to here was natural baldness, with no hair roots remaining in the skin. A dead scalp and a shaved face were to be the marks of judgment and humiliation.

In II Samuel 10 we read the story of the children of Ammon, who shaved off one-half of the beards of David's servants in order to mock and humiliate them. David, in response, advised them, "Tarry at Jericho until your beards be grown, and then return" (v. 5). It would have been easier and faster for them simply to have shaved off the other half of the beard, but since men normally had beards, a clean-shaven face would have made them even more conspicuous. Reference is made in the Bible to David's beard (I Sam. 21:13), Mephibosheth's beard (II Sam. 19:24), Aaron's beard (Ps. 133:2) and others.

Yet in numerous places mention is made of the use of razors and of the operation of shaving. There are 7 references to "razor" and 25 to "shave," "shaved" and "shaven." The question therefore arises: If men customarily wore beards, why would they have any need for razors? How could they wear beards and at the same time be shaved?

It is significant to note that in the Bible the razor is commonly spoken of as coming "upon the head." There was a distinctive mark for a Nazarite, a man who had separated himself to the Lord for a special purpose by a specific vow: "All the days of the vow of his separation there shall no razor come upon his head: until the days be fulfilled, in the which he separateth himself unto the Lord" (Num. 6:5).

Note also Judges 13:5; 16:17; and I Samuel 1:11. But if the Nazarite, by some inadvertent act, should defile himself and void his vow of consecration, his instructions were explicit: "Then he shall shave his head in the day of his cleansing, on the seventh day shall he shave it. And the Nazarite shall shave the head of his separation at the door of the tabernacle of the congregation, and shall take the hair of the head of his separation, and put it in the fire. And the priest shall take the sodden shoulder of the ram, and one unleavened cake out of the basket, and one unleavened wafer, and shall put them upon the hands of the Nazarite, after the hair of his separation is shaven" (Num. 6:9,18,19).

101

The inference seems clear: Normally all men shaved their heads; the Nazarite, who was set apart to God in a special way, refrained from doing so during the time he was under his vow.

Never will I forget the peculiar impression made on me when I first arrived on my chosen mission field in North Africa and found that the men all wore beards but kept their heads shaved! It seemed very strange because I was accustomed only to our Western culture, in which most men shave their faces and let the hair grow on their heads. A well-groomed man in North Africa would always wear attractive headgear in the presence of special guests and when he was outdoors. This has been the practice in Bible lands from time immemorial. When the men in the Middle East first saw Westerners with their faces shaved smooth and with a heavy growth of hair on their heads, they were no doubt equally surprised and shocked. After all, God has put hair on both the face and the head of a man; who is to say which place shall be shaved and which shall be trimmed?

The priests of ancient Israel, who were separate from the men of the other tribes, were required to be distinct in their dress and grooming habits. Therefore, the divine instruction given to them when they ministered in the holy temple was that they should *not* "shave their heads, nor suffer their locks to grow long; they shall only poll [trim] their heads" (Ezek. 44:20). Priests, being a distinct holy order, were neither to shave their heads like ordinary men nor to let their locks grow long like the Nazarites. They were simply to trim their hair. This marked them as being different from the

102

ordinary men of their time and singled them out as God's special servants.

It was normal practice for a common man, when engaging in any special worship or religious ritual, to change his garments and have his head freshly shaved. This would compare to the fact that most men in our day would not want to go to church wearing several days' growth of beard; rather, they would want to be freshly shaved and neatly groomed. In keeping with this, we note that the patriarch Job, when he "fell down upon the ground and worshipped" the Lord, first "shaved his head" (Job. 1:20). He also tore off his ordinary robe and donned a special garment of humiliation before God. The Apostle Paul did a similar thing when he went into the temple to take a vow in order to placate his Judaistic enemies. He cleansed himself and the men who joined him and had his head freshly shaved (Acts 21:23,24). This gives added significance to the statement in I Corinthians 11:14: "If a man have long hair [on his head], it is a shame unto him."

Chapter 26

Tentmaking

Some Christians are surprised and even disappointed when they learn that the great Apostle Paul was a tentmaker by trade. It seems incongruous that a learned man, such as he very evidently was, and such a towering Christian leader should have what they consider to be a rather demeaning occupation. Many are especially surprised that he continued in that occupation even after becoming an apostle and evangelist. That he did so is obvious from such passages as Acts 18:3; 20:34; I Thessalonians 2:9; and II Thessalonians 3:8.

To begin with, we must bear in mind that tents were very common dwelling places in Bible times. They still are, in many countries of the Near East. From the Old Testament we learn that Noah (Gen. 9:21) and Abraham (13:3,18; 18:1) lived in tents, as did Isaac (26:17,25) and Jacob (31:25; 33:18). Moses lived in a tent for many years (Ex. 18:7; 33:8,10). To this day, multitudes of people in those lands know no other shelter as home.

For this reason, tentmaking became a very popular and independent occupation in those countries. Special marketplaces were set up for the sale of tents and articles pertaining to tents and tent life.

It would be fair to compare tentmakers in Bible times to carpenters and masons in our day. Tentmaking, in fact, was held in higher esteem than our modern builders' occupations. I have been told that celebrated and learned men, even kings, preferred such an occupation to a life of idleness. It is said that a certain oriental king, after taking care of the matters of state during the day, would retire in the evening with his wife to a humble room in the palace where together they would work on tents and household items and secretly send these products to the marketplace for sale.

Another fact to keep in mind is that, in the time of Christ, every Jewish boy was taught some kind of craft or occupation that would enable him to earn a good living, regardless of what particular professional career he might choose. Thus, no matter what happened to that individual, or where he might be, he could always fall back on his craft to provide for himself and his family. This custom has been followed in many countries by various peoples, and I think it is a good one.

The Apostle Paul, though highly educated and trained for the rabbinical profession (and perhaps for the Sanhedrin) chose tentmaking as his trade. The choice was made either by himself as a boy or, more likely, by his father, who may himself have been a tentmaker, since the particular craft or trade of a father was frequently taken up by his sons.

Tents in the Near East today, as in ancient times, are made of strips of heavy materials just over a yard wide. Woven of goat or camel hair and

105

hemplike fiber, the material is usually made by women during spare time in their household routines. The raw materials are carded and then spun by means of a spindle. The cord thus spun is as thick as the heavy wrapping cord we use for tying parcels for shipment. It is wound into huge balls as it is spun.

The weaving is done in a very crude manner outside the tent, without the aid of a loom, though by a loomlike process. A kind of shuttle affair is passed back and forth, alternating between the cords that have been strung out as the warp of the material. When woven, the tent strips are about a quarter of an inch thick.

The tent is then actually "made" by sewing these strips together, producing the family residence. The tents are rectangular or oblong, never round or square. They vary in size according to the wealth of the man and the size of his family. There is usually a separating partition in the center to divide the space into "kitchen" and "living room" areas, the former generally serving as the women's compartment and the latter as the place for the men. This partition is formed either by suspending rugs or extra tent fabric or, more commonly, by stacking up the family supplies of grain and other produce, rugs, bundles of clothing, and the like.

Either carpets or straw mats are spread on the dirt floor for the people to sit on, especially when guests arrive. The more prominent the guest, the more luxurious the spread, depending, of course, on the wealth of the owner.

In dry weather the tents let through a great deal of sunlight, particularly when the materials are new, so during the first rain of the season, leakage is profuse. But as soon as the rains soak the material, it tightens up and the tent becomes virtually waterproof.

The actual work of the tentmaker in Paul's time probably involved the sewing of the strips of material together to form the tent itself and the adding of such appropriate accessories as tent ropes, poles and pegs. I assume that the apostle engaged exclusively in this part of the work. Certainly he did not do the actual weaving of the material, which was normally women's work.

It is the duty of each woman to weave one new strip of material for her tent annually. Then, during the dry season, with the aid of a professional tentmaker and the male members of her household, she opens the tent in the center, sews in the new strip, and discards the oldest strip at the outside edge. In this way she always keeps a roof over her family.

I have personally eaten, slept and lived weeks at a time in these tents, and I can testify that they are actually quite comfortable and appealing. There is nothing degrading or demeaning about living in such tents. Though menial, tentmaking is obviously not a "mean" occupation.

Chapter 27

Was Jesus Born in a Stable?

For many years, whenever I thought about Christ's birth in Bethlehem, a mental picture was automatically formed in my mind of a barn for cows and horses. There were many such barns in Minnesota, where I grew up on a farm. But my experience in the lands of the Near East, to the east and south of the Mediterranean, has since formed quite a different picture in my mind's eye.

First of all, we must remember that Bethlehem was a village in Judea, not far from Jerusalem, and ordinary farm animals would not normally have been sheltered within its borders. It is quite possible that a village dweller might have had a goat or two, or perhaps two or three sheep, or even a cow, but certainly there would have been no stable such as that usually pictured by Westerners inside a town like Bethlehem.

Stables for sheltering a herd of cattle or a flock of sheep to protect them from the elements evidently did not exist in Bible lands and times. The nearest thing to animal shelters were the sheep cotes, or "folds." For the most part, these were merely open enclosures, walled to protect the animals from thieves and beasts of prey rather than from the elements. The word "stable" appears only once in the Scriptures (Ezek. 25:5), and the words translated "barn" or "barns," occurring in the King James Version nine times, do not refer to buildings for animals but rather to storehouses for grain and produce.

In the Gospel of Luke we are told that the mother of Jesus, after giving birth to the Son of God, "wrapped him in swaddling clothes, and laid him in a manger" (2:7). Since the manger was the place from which the animals ate their food, it is quite natural for us Westerners to conclude that Jesus was born in a stable. But the significant statement of Luke is "Because there was no room for them in the inn." Joseph and Mary, as newly arrived travelers and, doubtless, complete strangers to Bethlehem, naturally went to a public inn for lodging. But they found that the inn was already filled with other travelers who had come to Bethlehem for the same purpose—government registration.

Since it was customary in those times to use animals in traveling, even if not actually in a full caravan, public inns found it essential to provide some kind of housing for the beasts as well as for the travelers themselves. Therefore, adjacent to, and usually connected with, the inn were such accommodations—not stables in the sense of common farm stables but like the older "livery stables" known to our fathers. Stories from the days of the stagecoaches remind us that wayside inns which provided food and lodging for people also had to provide food and shelter for the horses or the mules.

In the time of Christ, travelers often journeyed by camels and donkeys. And the inns of the day usually provided accommodations where the "keepers" of these animals could sleep near their beasts and their other possessions to guard them overnight. It was not uncommon, therefore, for the poorer working people to lodge in the animals' quarters along with their beasts of burden.

The guest rooms were already completely filled when Joseph and Mary arrived at the inn at Bethlehem that night. Therefore, even though Mary was "great with child" (v. 5) they had no choice but to spend the night in the section provided for animals, their keepers and the caravan servants. There, amid beasts and coarse male work-hands, Mary "brought forth her firstborn son" (v. 7), who in reality was God incarnate. It was indeed a very lowly, inconvenient and improper place for a baby to be born. It must have been very trying for Mary to deliver her child under such circumstances—physically distressing and socially humiliating—but that was a part of the price she, as the mother of the Saviour, had to pay to bring Him into the human family.

Luke says that "while they were there, . . . she brought forth her firstborn son" (vv. 6,7). This, of course, implies that He may not have been born the night of their arrival, as is commonly conjectured. Mary was "great with child" (v. 5) when they arrived, and they obviously had no intention of leaving Bethlehem until after the baby had been born and the mother was well enough to travel.

Chapter 28

The Palm Tree

In Psalm 92 we are told, "The righteous shall flourish like the palm tree" (v. 12).

The palm is a remarkable tree, and there are many respects in which it fittingly pictures the life and experience of a child of God.

Palm trees are widely noted for their unique beauty. Whether in primitive regions or in civilized lands, palm trees always stand out. They are beautiful in their natural state; they do not need the touch of human hands.

The Christian life, like the palm tree, should manifest true beauty—spiritual and moral. In fact, Psalm 90 says, "Let the beauty of the Lord our God be upon us" (v. 17). There are numerous references in the Psalms to the beauty of God's holiness, and it is this beauty that is to be reflected in our lives. If you are a Christian, the world has a right to expect some of the beauty of Jesus Christ and the beauty of God's holiness to be manifested in your life and daily walk. Obviously this is what the psalmist had in mind when he wrote: "The righteous shall flourish like the palm tree" (92:12).

The palm tree is beautiful, and so is the life of the Christian who is truly consecrated. The genuine

Christian character is the most beautiful character on earth, just as the palm tree is one of the most beautiful of all trees.

A striking fact about the palm tree is that it almost invariably grows erect and straight. Seldom do you see a crooked palm. When you see a palm tree that leans in a given direction, you can be sure it is due to some unnatural circumstance such as constant strong winds. This is not true of all species of trees by any means. Some are very crooked and gnarled, but the palm tree is, by its nature, upright, straight and erect.

The Christian life, pictured in God's Word, is a perfectly upright life. The Christian's life is not to be "crooked." It is to be straight and true at all times. The Christian's character is not to be gnarled, rough or twisted, causing men to scoff instead of to believe when they hear the believer's testimony for Jesus Christ.

Another remarkable thing about the palm tree is that its life is in the center, or the heart, of the tree. It is not at the circumference, under the bark, as is the case with most trees. The Christian life is like that. It does not consist of outward things but is a deep, inner, spiritual life. Indeed, a Christian is one in whose heart the Holy Spirit has implanted a new, divine life, making him a child of God.

The love of God is poured into the believer's heart by the Holy Spirit—love "which passeth knowledge" (Eph. 3:19). The Christian also has within his soul a joy that is "unspeakable and full of glory" (I Pet. 1:8) and a peace that passes human understanding (Phil. 4:7). All this is on the inside. The Christian is not to live by outward nourishment from the world but by the inner nourishment that comes from the Holy Spirit through the Word of God. This, too, is part of the meaning of the statement "The righteous shall flourish like the palm tree" (Ps. 92:12). The Christian life is a deep, sweet, rich life within.

The palm tree is master over virtually all circumstances. The palm flourishes even in barren desert areas where no other plant life can exist. There may not be a spear of grass or any other kind of foliage, yet in the barren sands of the desert you may see the beautiful and dignified palm tree, triumphant and erect. Drought, heat, blight, wind—no matter what may prevail, the palm tree triumphs. It is not dependent on such circumstances but is triumphant over them.

In this respect, too, this remarkable tree sets a pattern for the Christian's life. The man of God should, like the palm tree, flourish and be triumphant over all circumstances—wind, storm, drought or deluge. The Christian is always to remain steadfast because he is nourished by an inner life rather than by outward circumstances.

Palm trees and branches have long been used around the world as symbols of victory. Triumphant armies in and before the days of the Roman Empire carried palm branches when they returned from victories in battle. Since the palm tree is itself a victorious, triumphant tree, triumphing over drought and other difficult circumstances, it is a fitting symbol of victory in human life.

This symbolism of the palm tree is apparent in various parts of the Scriptures. When Jesus made his triumphal entry into the city of Jerusalem, the people "took branches of palm trees, and went

113

forth to meet him, and cried, Hosanna: Blessed is the King of Israel that cometh in the name of the Lord" (John 12:13). And in the seventh chapter of the Book of the Revelation the final victory of the saints is portrayed by this description: "[They were] clothed with white robes, and palms in their hands; and [they] cried with a loud voice, saying, Salvation to our God which sitteth upon the throne, and unto the Lamb" (vv. 9,10).

The Bible certainly has much to say about the Christian life as a life of triumph. We are to be triumphant and victorious over all the circumstances that may oppose us in this world. There are battles, there are seasons of drought, and there are storms, but in all this we have the inner life and power of the Lord Jesus Christ. Therefore, we can always triumph in Him (Rom. 8:37; I Cor. 15:57; II Cor. 2:14).

Palm trees are nourished from springs of water hidden beneath the surface of the earth. This is the reason they can grow in dry and barren desert territory. They have large, deep roots, and those roots go many feet into the earth until they find water for nurture. This hidden source is the secret of their triumph.

This is precisely the secret of the Christian life: We are not nourished by the outward things of the world but by a secret spring of living water—the Holy Spirit, who is dwelling within us and strengthening our inner man.

Jesus promised, "Whosoever drinketh of the water that I shall give him shall never thirst; but the water that I shall give him shall be in him a well of water springing up into everlasting life" (John 4:14; see also John 6:35; Eph. 3:16). Because

Christians are nourished from that hidden, secret spring, they can be triumphant and flourishing like the palm tree in the desert.

The palm tree is benevolent to mankind. In its shadow weary and worn desert travelers find rest and refreshment from the burning heat of their journey. Palm trees often mark the oases in the desert where travelers may find water. The coconut palm produces both food and drink for the hungry and thirsty. In some areas of the world people depend on the palm tree for their very existence. The date palm, of course, produces the sweet and nourishing fruit called "dates."

Palm oil has had many uses since primitive times and is still used.

Palms are used for constructing houses and other buildings in areas where these trees flourish, providing both the framework and the covering.

The sago palm produces in the upper part of its trunk a food substance which is both tasty and nourishing.

In all these respects we, as Christians, are to be like the palm tree. The verse we have been considering, "The righteous shall flourish like the palm tree" (Ps. 92:12), conveys both a divine exhortation and a divine expectation. Beauty, uprightness, inner life and strength, mastery over circumstances, nourishment from the divine Source and benevolence to mankind—all these are to be the manifestations of the true Christian life.

Animals
of the
Bible

Chapter 29

Unusual Animals

A great many animals are named and identified in the Bible. In addition to these, there are some which we cannot positively identify and some which we know little about. Some of these are mentioned a number of times and others, seldom. Even a firsthand knowledge of Bible lands cannot clear up the questions about some of these creatures. They may once have abounded in that part of the world, but they are no longer found there.

One unusual name applied to a Bible animal is "behemoth." When the Lord revealed himself to the patriarch Job in His great power and sovereignty, one of the things He said was "Behold now behemoth, which I made with thee; he eateth grass as an ox. Lo now, his strength is in his loins, and his force is in the navel of his belly. He moveth his tail like a cedar. . . . His bones are as strong pieces of brass; his bones are like bars of iron. He lieth under the shady trees, in the covert of the reed, and fens. The shady trees cover him with their shadow. . . . Behold, he drinketh up a river, and hasteth not: he trusteth that he can draw up

119

Jordan into his mouth. . . . His nose pierceth through snares" (Job 40:15-18,21-24).

The name "behemoth" does not identify this animal, because the Hebrew word *behemah*, as now commonly used, does not designate any specific animal but simply signifies "beast." Hence, we are left to the description in Job 40 to determine exactly what animal was meant.

Many Bible dictionaries and commentaries take the behemoth to be the hippopotamus. The chief arguments for this are the great weight and the great strength alluded to in the Book of Job, as well as the animal's love of rivers and water.

My own opinion is that the Bible behemoth was the elephant. The Book of Job makes special mention of the tail (v. 17); the elephant has a much larger tail than the hippo, so it fits the description better. The repeated mention of ivory in the Bible indicates the presence of elephants and the practice of elephant hunting. Solomon built his throne in the great Jerusalem temple using solid ivory and gold (I Kings 10:18; II Chron. 9:17).

In the Book of Ezekiel "horns of ivory" are referred to, and I feel they mean the tusks of the elephant (Ezek. 27:15). We know that the Arabs (Ishmaelites) did an extensive trade in ivory long before the time of Christ, perhaps as early as the days of Joseph.

In the description given in the Book of Job, the behemoth's great strength is referred to, and this, too, seems to fit the elephant better than the hippopotamus. The reference to his nose piercing through snares well describes the elephant's use of his trunk when trapped in the great nets sometimes used for capturing him.

The word "unicorn" is of Latin origin. Its literal meaning is "one horn," indicating a creature thus endowed by nature. In ancient mythology such an animal is visualized as having a body and head like a horse, the hind legs of a stag, the tail of a lion, and a single pretentious horn protruding from the middle of the forehead.

However, only in the King James Version of the Bible is the word "unicorn" found. Elsewhere, the Hebrew word *reem* is rendered "wild ox." *Reem* does not signify a one-horned beast at all; rather, it indicates the animal now known as the "wild ox." This creature, technically known as the "aurochs," was once plentiful in both Europe and Palestine. It is a huge animal, standing up to 6 feet high at the shoulders, a voracious eater and exceptionally powerful. This animal was well known to the people of Old Testament lands, but it was untamable and impossible to use for agriculture.

The creature named "leviathan" in the Old Testament is mentioned in four places: Job 41:1; Psalm 74:14; 104:26; Isaiah 27:1. In each instance the word is used without the article, indicating that it was likely used as a kind of proper name rather than simply as a noun. This would indicate that the animal referred to had a prominent place in the thinking of people in Old Testament times. "Leviathan" may have been a kind of household word to them.

The Hebrew word *livyathan* signifies a huge water animal. Job 41 indicates that the leviathan inhabited the water: "Canst thou draw out leviathan with an hook?" (v. 1). In Psalm 104 leviathan is described as traveling with ships, further indicating a creature of the water. Together, the clues given in the four passages where "leviathan" is mentioned suggest that this creature was the crocodile.

"Conies" are referred to four times in the Old Testament (Lev. 11:5; Deut. 14:7; Ps. 104:18; and Prov. 30:26). These passages indicate that the coney was a small animal which chewed the cud and was a rock dweller. In Deuteronomy 14:7 the coney is described as being distinct from the rabbit though definitely like it in certain respects. Unlike the rabbit, it had short legs and ears and no tail. This little creature is now called the "hyrax."

In various respects these little animals may be compared to the prairie dogs of the midwestern United States, although they had very different feet. The coney's feet have been described as being "tiny, but elephantlike"; therefore, conies have been called "little cousins of the elephant." However, such descriptions can be very misleading, and I cite them with caution.

The coney was a timid but extremely active little animal, making its home in rocky territory and particularly in rocky knolls or hills. He was strictly a vegetarian. While his jaw action resembled cud-chewing, he did not have the kind of digestive tract that cud-chewing animals normally have, and therefore he should not really be classed among them.

Solomon drew a wise and practical lesson from this little creature when he said, "The conies are but a feeble folk, yet make they their houses in the rocks" (Prov. 30:26). In the spiritual realm, this reminds us of the words of Jesus in Matthew 7:24,25. Here He compared those who heard and obeyed His words to a man who built his house on the rock instead of on the sand.

The hart was a small variety of deer like the little red deer now found in Syria and in parts of Africa and Europe. It was similar to the American deer but much smaller. The name "hart" was usually applied to the male animal after it has reached the age of five years. At this time it had six-pronged antlers, which were shed annually like those of American deer. The meat of the hart and of the hind, the female animal, was highly prized among those who lived in the Middle East.

"Then shall the lame man leap as an hart, and the tongue of the dumb sing: for in the wilderness shall waters break out, and streams in the desert" (Isa. 35:6). This simile indicates the fleet-footedness and the capacity this slight animal had for making long jumps. The psalmist's statement, "He maketh my feet like hinds' feet, and setteth me upon my high places" (Ps. 18:33), bears out the same idea, as does Habakkuk 3:19.

The most striking reference to the hart is Psalm 42:1,2: "As the hart panteth after the water brooks, so panteth my soul after thee, O God. My soul thirsteth for God, for the living God." Though the hart was a small animal, it required a great amount of water. The two things it always sought were good pastures and streams of fresh water from which it could drink many times each day. Some Hebrew scholars believe the brooks of this passage actually signify aqueducts. This adds another rich thought to the passage.

Two spiritual lessons for us from the hart are that God satisfies our constant spiritual thirst and that He enables our feet to be swift to do His will.

There are about 35 occurrences of the words "dragon" and "dragons" in the King James Version of the Scriptures. In the Old Testament, the Hebrew word signifies a long, serpentlike creature. In some instances, at least, it probably indicates a member of the crocodile family. The reference in Jeremiah 51:34, "He hath swallowed me up like a dragon," strongly suggests the action of a crocodile.

In the New Testament, the word "dragon" appears only in the Book of the Revelation. The dragons seen in John's visions here were not necessarily real animals, for numerous creatures appeared throughout the apocalyptic vision that were unlike any animals that we know to have existed.

The dragon of Revelation is definitely associated with the Devil. In the Scriptures Satan is identified with the serpent (Gen. 3:1-15; Rev. 20:2), the dragon (Rev. 20:2), the lion (I Pet. 5:8) and the dog (Ps. 22:20). In the mythology of several ancient pagan religions the dragon was used as a symbol of the Evil One, who opposed all righteous deeds. The symbolism was doubtless carried over from the spiritual knowledge their ancestors once possessed (Rom. 1:21-25).

The bear referred to in the Bible is the one now known as the Syrian brown bear. This beast still lives in Palestine—a hairy, shaggy creature, strong and cruel. It was used in prophetic Scripture to symbolize the great power and notorious cruelty of the Medo-Persian Empire which would conquer and devour Babylon (Dan. 7:5). Prophecy students also see a reference here to the "Russian bear" of end-time events.

124

Chapter 30

The Donkey

The ass, or donkey, is mentioned more than 150 times in the Bible. This fact indicates how common it was in Bible times and in Bible lands. No other domesticated animal is referred to as often.

The implications usually drawn in our day concerning this animal appear to be faulty when we know more about its real place in life in Bible times. The ass was not looked upon as a downgraded beast, and to ride on one did not indicate condescension or humiliation. On the contrary, to ride a "white ass" was a definite sign of respect and dignity (Judg. 5:10; 12:14). Those who possessed donkeys had high social standing in the community.

It is significant that Abraham, who is described in Scripture as being "very rich in cattle, in silver, and in gold" (Gen. 13:2), "rose up early in the morning, and saddled his ass" (22:3) when he was commanded by God to sacrifice Isaac on Mount Moriah.

Of one of the judges in Israel we read: "Jair, a Gileadite, . . . judged Israel twenty and two years. And he had thirty sons that rose on thirty ass colts, and they had thirty cities" (Judg. 10:3,4). These men were the highest rulers in the land at that time.

Achsah, the daughter of prominent Caleb, rode an ass when she approached her father to ask a favor (Judg. 1:14). So did Abigail, the wife of wealthy Nabal (I Sam. 25:23).

The number of donkeys a man possessed was often the measure of his wealth. Job, for example, is described as a great and affluent man, having "seven thousand sheep, and three thousand camels, and five hundred yoke of oxen, and five hundred she asses, and a very great household" (Job 1:3). The Bible records that on one occasion of triumph over the Midianites the men of Israel captured 61,000 asses (Num. 31:32-34).

As saddle animals, asses apparently were preferred by officials and prominent men for normal, peaceful travel. Horses were regarded as steeds of war and were not often used in domestic and social life. The ass is naturally better for riding and carrying loads because it is more surefooted on rugged trails.

One particular incident in connection with the ass comes to the Bible reader's mind. It is Jesus' triumphal entry into the city of Jerusalem (Matt. 21:1-11). That this royal journey would be made on a donkey was prophesied years earlier by Zechariah: "Behold, thy King cometh . . . riding upon an ass, and upon a colt the foal of an ass" (Zech. 9:9). It is generally thought that Jesus' riding a young ass on that occasion signified great humiliation and lowliness. But if this imagery had been in the minds of the people, would they have hailed Him King and shouted, "Hosanna to the son

126

of David . . . ; Hosanna in the highest" (Matt. 21:9)?

The word "lowly" in the prophecy of Zechariah simply indicated meekness. It signified that the Messiah's mission was to be one of peace rather than one of vengeance and judgment. In quoting the prophecy of Zechariah, Matthew interpreted the word "lowly" as "meek," a word which means "mild, submissive, gentle, or moderate." The prophet also mentioned that the coming King would be just and that He would bring salvation.

Using the donkey as a symbol, Jesus was telling the people that He had not come to stir up insurrection and rebellion against Rome, though this was what most of them hoped and desired. Instead, He had come on a mission of peace to the souls of men.

Whereas the horse usually symbolized warfare, the donkey represented tranquillity and peace. This was especially true from the time of the reign of Solomon onward.

Anyone who has made much use of a donkey will concede that it is not a particularly stubborn or stupid animal, but on the whole it is quite a docile, wise and reliable creature.

One evening in North Africa I was walking with an Arab shepherd who was bringing his little flock of livestock home to his tent for the night. I asked him, "Who created these animals?" The prompt Islamic reply was, "Allah [God] did."

"Why did Allah create them?" I asked. The shepherd quickly answered, "He created them to serve man."

"I agree with you," I said. "I, too, believe that God made these creatures to serve man. And they are all doing it. They are doing what God made them to do. They are fulfilling His divine will for their existence. But now let me ask you one more question. Why did God create *man*?"

The shepherd looked puzzled and uncertain. After some hesitation he said rather slowly, "I don't know."

"Well, let me tell you. God created human beings to honor and glorify Him by living holy lives, and also to enjoy fellowship with Him now and forever."

With much solemnity the shepherd replied, "Sir, I believe you are right. That must be the reason God made man."

"Are men doing this?" was my next question.

"No," came the reply. "Men are not honoring God in their lives. They are doing many evil things contrary to God's holy will."

"What about you?" I queried.

"No," he admitted, "I am not honoring or pleasing God in my life either. Like all others, I am following the ways of Satan."

I then said, "Is it not sad that all creation does God's will except the noblest creature He has made—man? We have agreed that even the burros are fulfilling God's will for them! Yet man, God's highest creature, rebels and refuses to submit to God."

Chapter 31

The Dog

The Bible speaks more highly of the ass than do most people of our day, but in the case of the dog, quite the opposite is true. While dogs are often household pets and the subjects of much pampering and doting in our world, in biblical days most dogs were despised.

An early Scottish missionary to the Near East once described dogs in this way: "They are of wolflike appearance, black or tawny yellow in color, mangy and unclean. They are tolerated . . . because they devour the family refuse . . . and act as sanitary officers without payment." My own experience bears out this description. These dogs are largely scavengers, eating anything they can find or any piece of garbage tossed to them.

But there are basically two kinds of dogs included in the statements of the Bible. The ones most frequently referred to have just been described—the vicious, short-haired creatures originally derived from wolf stock, which are very wolflike in nature and action. These animals jealously guard their owner's house or tent and fiercely bark at all approaching strangers. They will also viciously attack unless they are called off by their masters. I was frequently frightened when visiting Arab tents because of this, and usually I carried a handful of rocks to protect myself. Rocks are the only things these dogs fear and respect.

The second kind of dog mentioned in the Bible is less common—the shepherd's dog. Job referred to these, saying, "Now they that are younger than I have me in derision, whose fathers I would have disdained to have set with the dogs of my flock" (Job. 30:1). He indicated higher esteem for his shepherd dogs than for the men he was describing. These shepherd dogs were feared, but they were not necessarily despised by all the people; in fact, they were prized. The shepherds themselves likely regarded their dogs as personal companions. Sometimes these shepherd dogs were trained to help corral the sheep when they strayed, but primarily they were to protect the livestock from wild beasts or thieves and to give warning at night of the approach of intruders. Hence, shepherd dogs were valuable to their owners and served a useful purpose.

But since the first dogs described were the commonly known type, it is understandable why they were despised by the people and held to be unclean by the Law of Moses. The name "dog" was sometimes given to a man who had lost all regard for modesty and moral principles. The term was often used to designate a man who had involved himself in such an abomination as sodomy, the most repulsive form of homosexuality. Note this association in Deuteronomy 23:17,18: "There shall be no whore of the daughters of Israel, nor a sodomite of the sons of Israel. Thou shalt not bring the hire of a whore, or the price of a dog, into the house of the Lord thy God for any vow: for even both these are an abomination unto the Lord thy God."

In Psalm 22:20 David prophetically uttered one of the prayers Christ prayed during the time He hung on the cross, obviously comparing the dog with the Devil. In the next verse he said, "Save me from the lion's mouth," and we know from the New Testament that Satan is compared to a roaring lion (I Pet. 5:8). Dogs were indeed commonly associated with the Devil in the minds of the ancient Israelites.

Christ's human persecutors were also prophetically designated as "dogs" by the psalmist: "For dogs have compassed me" (Ps. 22:16).

Unfaithful religious leaders and false teachers are similarly designated in the Scripture: "His watchmen are blind: they are all ignorant, they are all dumb dogs, they cannot bark; sleeping, lying down, loving to slumber. Yea, they are greedy dogs which can never have enough" (Isa. 56:10,11). In a similar vein the Apostle Paul wrote: "Beware of dogs, beware of evil workers, beware of the concision" (Phil. 3:2). Jesus likened evil and unholy men to dogs when He said, "Give not that which is holy unto the dogs" (Matt. 7:6). The imagery and similes used in the Bible conveyed obvious meaning to the people living in Bible times, but because the experiences of our lives are so vastly different from theirs, we often miss these meanings.

Chapter 32

The Lion

The lion is a familiar animal in the Bible. There are about 200 references to "the king of the beasts" in both Testaments, most of them in the Old Testament.

Special mention is made of his great strength (Judg. 14:18; II Sam. 1:23; Prov. 30:30); his terrible ferocity (Ps. 7:2; 17:12; 22:13; Jer. 2:30; Nah. 2:12); and his frightening roar (Prov. 19:12; 20:2; Isa. 5:29; Ezek. 22:25; Amos 3:8; I Pet. 5:8).

The two qualities which probably have had the greatest influence in giving the lion the title "king of beasts" are his swiftness and great strength. The elephant, rhinoceros and hippopotamus are larger and stronger than the lion, but they are clumsy and not fleet-footed like the lion.

"And Caleb said, He that smiteth Kirjath-sepher, and taketh it, to him will I give Achsah my daughter to wife. And Othniel, the son of Kenaz, Caleb's younger brother, took it: and he gave him Achsah his daughter to wife" (Judg. 1:12,13).

Kirjath-sepher was a strongly fortified city. It was fortified on the outside and well defended by the army on the inside. The men of Judah had captured place after place, city after city, but when they came to Kirjath-sepher nobody wanted to risk trying to take it. When he saw that no one was willing to attack the city, Caleb, their leader, threw out a challenge, promising that whoever would take the city would have his daughter Achsah to be his wife.

The man Othniel accepted the challenge. "Othniel" means "lion of God," and the name suited him well. He led a troop of bold fighters against the city and with his lionlike nature he took it. His bold adventure displayed great strength and great swiftness. He showed himself true to his name.

Long after Othniel had so valiantly and courageously demonstrated his strength in capturing the city of Kirjath-sepher, he observed the spiritual apostasy of his people and saw how as a consequence they had come under the domination of a heathen king. He responded to the call of God to lead an army to deliver them, and with great strength and speed he gloriously delivered his people. He liberated them from the iron hand of the heathen king of Mesopotamia and became the first of the rulers of Israel known as the "judges." Under his rule of 40 years the land had rest and security.

"Othniel" signifies not only a lion but "lion *of God*." He was a man who truly knew God in a personal way—a man who trusted God. Any man who learns to trust God can be as strong as a lion!

Othniel was incensed by the apostasy of his people and by their bondage to pagan gods and rulers. Under the direction of God's Spirit, and in His strength, he fought against this wickedness.

No man can triumph in the crises of life unless he knows God and derives his strength from Him. The great Apostle Paul said, "I can do all things through Christ which strengtheneth me" (Phil. 4:13).

Some men are lions of the Devil; some are lions of God. What about you? Does the name "Othniel" fit you? Are you a lion of God?

Chapter 33

The Camel

Camels are referred to throughout much of the Bible. The early Hebrew patriarchs possessed many camels and made frequent use of them. Abraham's affluence is signified by the fact that "he had sheep, and oxen, and he asses, . . . and she asses, and camels" (Gen. 12:16). Likewise, Jacob "had much cattle, . . . and camels, and asses" (30:43). Job's prestige and wealth are indicated by the fact that he possessed "seven thousand sheep, and three thousand camels, and five hundred yoke of oxen, and five hundred she asses, and a very great household; so that this man was the greatest of all the men of the east" (Job 1:3).

After Israel had settled in the land of Canaan, the use of camels was not so common. But it is evident that the camel was still a familiar beast in the land until the time of the New Testament. We are told that John the Baptist wore "raiment of camel's hair" (Matt. 3:4), and Jesus drew some striking similes in connection with the beast (Matt. 19:24; 23:24).

Let us notice some of the characteristics of the camel and learn from them some practical lessons for everyday Christian living.

E. W. Rice said, "He is a cold-blooded, heavy, sullen animal, having little feeling and little susceptibility for pain. Thistles and briars and thorns he crops and chews with more avidity than the softest green fodder; nor does he seem to feel pain from blows or pricks, unless they are very violent" (*Orientalisms in Bible Lands*, p. 193). I have marveled at the way camels devour and subsist on coarse, prickly shrubs of the desert as though they were delicious morsels.

It is this unusual characteristic of physical endurance that makes the camel such a valuable beast of burden and transportation in the desert areas. The desert nomad and his camel are seen as an almost inseparable team in the Near East.

Here is a significant lesson for the Christian: Regardless of what the outward circumstances of life may be and regardless of how barren a spiritual desert the Christian lives and works in, he need not fall or succumb to temptation (see I Cor. 4:11-13; II Cor. 4:8-12; 11:1-30; Heb. 11:32-40).

By the way they carry their heads erect, camels leave one with an unforgettable impression of defiance toward all other creatures, including humans. I have never seen a camel—under any circumstance—hang or "droop" his head. He seems to be constantly alert to everything around him. He is completely unaffected by things which cause other creatures to grow weary and wilt. Neither distance nor heat nor heavy load causes the camel to betray defeat or fatigue by the posture of his head. In this characteristic he is unique among all creatures, including man.

136

What a lesson this should be to the Christian! Note Psalm 3:3; Luke 21:28; Hebrews 12:1-12; James 4:10.

Camels have been called "ships of the desert." It is well known that a camel can travel for many hours—even days—without food or water. It would be safe to say that a camel can go seven or eight days without nourishment or hydration.

Every person who knows the camel's capacity to live and travel for long periods of time without replenishing his supply of food and water has wondered how he is nourished and sustained.

In his body the camel has a series of cells, or sacks, in which water is stored. To fill them he consumes as much as nine or ten gallons of water at a single drink of a few minutes' duration. This inward labyrinth of organic chasms or successive stomachs will supply him with water for several days' journey. When caravans run out of water, a camel will sometimes be killed to extract water from its stomachs to save people's lives.

The camel's hump contains another hidden source of nutrient supply. Before a long journey, camels are fed as much as possible by their owners, and a fatty matter is accumulated in the hump to provide a reserve to be utilized as needed on his journey. At the beginning of the journey, the camel's hump is normally very large and quite soft with this partially digested food. When he returns from his journey the hump is small. In fact, it may be only an empty bag of skin hanging from his back.

Here, too, is a lesson for the Christian. He is sustained in the trials and temptations of life because he is able to "store up" in his soul nourishment from the Word of God and fellowship with God. Psalm 1 is a striking example of this, especially verses 2 and 3. Note also Psalm 119:11, 15, 16, 49, 50, 60-62; Ephesians 3:16; Colossians 1:11.

A characteristic which is a great asset to the camel is his surefootedness. He can travel with apparent ease and safety up and down the most formidable mountain slopes. He does not choose the path of least resistance when the going is tough, as a horse or a mule does, but seems instead to tread all the more surely and is rarely known to slip or stumble.

The spiritual lesson is easily discernible. We need more Christians who can maintain a balanced walk. Note such passages as Psalm 37:24; 40:2; 116:8; Proverbs 3:23,24; Jude 1:24.

The camel is naturally a common beast of burden for desert dwellers. But because the beast is so tall, he is difficult to load or to mount. So he is taught to kneel to receive his burden, whether it be a passenger or some commodity. He first bends his forelegs and falls upon his knees and then gradually settles down so that finally his breast lies solidly on the ground. A wooden frame, or saddle, usually made of cypress wood, spans his back, being girded tightly to him with either ropes or thin leather straps.

Having received his load, the camel rises to his feet by reversing the process he used in kneeling down. To me there seems to be a gesture of humility and submission on the part of the camel as he kneels to have his burden placed or removed.

Who can miss the spiritual lesson? When the trials of life are laid on us, or when the hand of

God places some special load or burden on us, we must kneel in submission under His sovereign hand to accept the burden, asking Him for strength and grace to bear it. The Christian must learn to submissively receive his burdens on his knees before God rather than to resist or shirk those burdens and responsibilities.

It is equally impressive to watch the camel at the close of his day's journey—as he kneels down again to discharge his burden. After a long, hot journey, carrying a heavy load, the beast kneels with grace and dignity to be unloaded at sundown. While witnessing this process, one can almost sense his feeling of relief from the load (see Gen. 24:11).

The Christian who must submissively kneel to accept his burdens must also learn to kneel for release. At the close of day, when the going has been hard and the burden heavy, what a relief it is to kneel down before our Heavenly Father and find relief from the toil and heat of the day! When we rest in His presence, we receive the benefits of physical rest and sleep and are given renewed strength to kneel again the next day to receive new burdens and responsibilities. Note such passages as Ephesians 3:13-16; Philippians 4:13; Hebrews 4:14-16.

Another outstanding characteristic of the camel is his constant, steady gait. From morning till night, mile after mile, yes, day after day, the camel continues his journey at a fixed, steady pace. Though some varieties of camels can run very fast and are sometimes even used for racing, the ordinary camel does not particularly like to run. Neither does he poke along at an extremely slow pace. He has a steady gait that can always be relied on.

Here, too, the application is easily understood. Some Christians plunge and dash, but they are soon exhausted and fall by the wayside. Others are always lagging behind, plodding at tortoise speed. They never really seem to get going for God. Between these two extremes is the kind of Christian God wants—one who "shall walk, and not faint" (Isa. 40:31). It is the steady Christian that produces fruit for God. It is the steady worker in the church that achieves things. It is the steady missionary on the mission field who can endure all the discouragements and oppositions and keep forging ahead. May God grant to us all the steady, unceasing pace of the faithful camel.

Scripture Index

141